DISCIPLE-SHIP:

The Price and the Prize

SO-BEZ-497

DISCIPLE-SHIP:
The Price and the Prize

JACK MAYHALL

Though this book is designed for the reader's personal enjoyment, it is also intended for group study. A Leader's Guide with Victor Multiuse Transparency Masters is available from your local bookstore or from the publisher.

VICTOR

BOOKS a division of SP Publications, Inc.
WHEATON. ILLINOIS 60187

Offices also in
Whitby, Ontario, Canada
Amersham-on-the-Hill, Bucks, England

Unless otherwise noted, Scripture quotations in this book are from the *New International Version* (NIV), © 1978 by the New York International Bible Society. Other quotations are from the *King James Version* (KJV); the *New American Standard Bible* (NASB), © 1960, 1962, 1963, 1968, 1971, 1972, 1973 by the Lockman Foundation, La Habra, California; the *Revised Standard Version* (RSV), Old Testament © 1952 and New Testament © 1946 by Division of Christian Education of the National Council of Christ in the United States of America; *The Living Bible* (TLB), © 1971 by Tyndale House; the *Amplified Bible* (AMP), © 1965 by Zondervan Publishing House; Phillips' *New Testament in Modern English* (PH), © 1958, 1959, 1960 by J.B. Phillips, published by The Macmillan Co.

Recommended Dewey Decimal Classification: 248.5
    Suggested Subject Heading: WITNESS-BEARING

Library of Congress Catalog Card Number: 83-51303
ISBN: 0-88207-110-6

© 1984 by SP Publications, Inc. All rights reserved
Printed in the United States of America

VICTOR BOOKS
A division of SP Publications, Inc.
        Wheaton, Illinois 60187

Contents

To Mother and Dad

With great appreciation for your
Encouragement
Prayer
and Love
through the years

Introduction

During a brief respite in an incredibly busy day for both of us, I found my wife Carole busily ironing. I said in amazement, "You are ambitious!"

She didn't even look up as she grimly responded, "I took a look at your side of the closet and discovered you were almost out of shirts. My ironing isn't *ambition*. It's *determination!*"

Ambition is defined as "a strong desire to gain a particular objective." Ambition is "zealous, eager, desirous, ardent, avid." At times we feel none of those things. It is then we need determination—the quality of being resolute—to have a firmness of purpose. Determination is perseverance when one *isn't* eager; it is tenacity in the face of a lack of zealousness; it is persistence when one doesn't feel ardent or avid. When ambition lies dead in the dust, determination forces us to proceed.

Both desire and determination are integral parts of the Christian life. There are periods when we are flooded with love for God and others; seasons of abounding joy in the Spirit; times of compassion for the souls of people. But there are also intervals in our Christian lives when we just "hang on." We lose our zealousness, our ardor, our eagerness. But deep down in our souls, God gives strength and determination to keep on keeping on in the race set before us.

Today we seem to hear two messages concerning the Christian life. One says "rest." The other says, "wrestle." I am convinced the two should marry—that the Christian life is "resting *and* wrestling."

Paul wrote, "We *wrestle* not against flesh and blood, but [we wrestle] against principalities and powers" (Eph. 6:12, KJV). Now that is quite a wrestling match! While it is true that it is Christ *in us* who gives the victory, we are told to "fight the good fight" (1 Tim. 6:12). So He uses our hands to hold His sword. And if our hands are not willing, we fall in defeat.

Paul also wrote, "Be *strong* [a command—something that we are to do] in the grace that is in Christ Jesus" [His part—giving us the grace to rest, 2 Tim. 2:1]. And the writer of Hebrews tells us, *"Strive* to enter that *rest"* (Heb. 4:11, RSV).

A paradox? To us perhaps. To God, definitely not. It is as true as the old saying, "Work as though it all depended on you. Pray as though it all depended on God."

Exactly.

Recently, I have been struck by Scriptures concerned with these things we are to do *ourselves* in living the Christian life. God commands us to train *ourselves* in godliness, to humble *ourselves* under His mighty hand, to deny *ourselves*, to delight *ourselves*, plus about 20 other commands that we are to do *ourselves*. We *determine* to do these things by acts of our will—from sheer obedience to His commands. Of course it is only through His Holy Spirit that we are able, but nonetheless our wills can either channel or block His power.

This book is an attempt to give balance to some thoughts floating around the Christian world today between "the God who does" and "the We who *will* to let Him."

Acknowledgment

Without the encouragement, inspiration, and hard work of Carole, my talented and wonderful wife, this book would never have come into existence. The original idea of this book was hers; most of the editing, writing, and rewriting was hers. Her diligence and faithfulness was a constant motivation to me. Hers is the labor of love. But I must accept full responsibility for the concepts and ideas in the content. We both pray it will be of some small help to you as you deepen your life in Christ.

—Jack Mayhall

1

Train Yourself in Godliness

I braked for a stoplight and glanced at the bumper sticker on the car stopped ahead of me. In bold black letters it declared, BALD IS BEAUTIFUL. Recently I had seen one stating, FAT IS BEAUTIFUL. *Now,* I thought, *all we need is one saying,* FIFTY IS BEAUTIFUL.

Yes, I was turning 50. Near that birthday, someone told me that the six ages of man are (1) beef broth, (2) ground steak, (3) sirloin, (4) filet mignon, (5) ground steak, and (6) beef broth. But the six ages of women are (1) infant, (2) little girl, (3) young miss, (4) young woman, (5) young woman, and (6) young woman.

It has been said that middle age is when you are just as young as you always were but it takes a lot more effort. But I really didn't feel old as I turned 50. I was inclined to agree with Victor Hugo who said, "Forty is the old age of youth; 50 is the youth of old age." I was looking forward to the next years of my life and while turning 50 was somewhat thought-provoking, I had a positive feeling about it. Oh, I felt some creakiness in a few joints, but during the 8 to 10 months before I became 50, that creakiness was overshadowed by the Lord beginning an unusual work in my heart. He caused me to ponder the question, "How am I going to invest the next 15 to 20 years of my life?"

Life Verses

Never before this time had I had what I considered to be a "life verse." God had given many promises through the years so it wasn't something I had especially longed for. But every once in a while I'd meet someone who had a life verse and I'd think, *That's nice. Wish I had one.* Every December I'd read my Bible diligently, searching for a verse just for the next year, but no one single verse or passage ever really impressed itself on me—until the year I turned 50.

At that time, one passage began to hammer away at my mind. It was uncanny how many people around me would use part or all of this passage. And frequently, as I reviewed various Scriptures, this one would stand out in a special way. I finally realized that after all this time, God was giving me a verse and a half, not just for the next year but for the rest of my life! It is found in 1 Timothy 4:7b-8: "Train yourself in godliness; for while bodily training is of some value, godliness is of value in every way, as it holds promise for the present life and also for the life to come" (RSV).

I'm excited about this! The more I delve into this passage, the more meaning God gives me. To fathom its depths—to research it and to put it into practice—is going to take the rest of my life because training oneself in godliness is not a one-semester course. It literally will require all of my remaining years.

Train

This passage says to "train yourself" and to do the training in two areas—godliness and physical fitness.

The word "train" in Greek is *gumnazō* from which the words

"gymnasium" and "gymnastics" come. It means to exercise and train the body or mind. Greek scholar Ellicott says it means "strenuous effort or exercise is involved." And this verse says I am to train *myself.* It is my responsibility. God has put the burden of getting this kind of training squarely on my shoulders.

One area in which we are to train ourselves is in physical fitness, for "bodily exercise is of some value." I do appreciate Paul putting in this little blurb about physical fitness. He prods me a bit here and I need that.

A friend in the Philippines wrote recently, "Many of you know that Ron trained in 1981 to run a marathon. He said, 'My goal is to finish alive and, if I do that, I would like to do it under four hours.' On November 21, he completed the marathon in 3 hours and 59 minutes. One important lesson related to training came out of this. Over the year Ron ran 1,316 miles to train for this 26-mile race. It took about 164 hours of preparation for 4 hours of running."

Every year Colorado Springs sponsors a 10-mile race. The runners go through the Garden of the Gods, into Manitou Springs, and back again. There isn't any money involved or even much publicity except locally, but it attracts a horde of runners each year.

I don't know anyone who really pushes to prepare for this race. No one gets another up early and goes out to run with him. It is up to each participant to ignite his own initiative and train himself to run and finish that race.

Win

Each year as they run, I am reminded of 1 Corinthians 9:24-25: "Do you not know that in a race all the runners run, but only one gets the prize? Run in such a way as to get the prize. Everyone who competes in the games goes into strict training. They do it to get a crown that will not last; but we do it to get a crown that will last forever."

A number of years ago Lorne Sanny, our Navigator President, preached a message on "How Can a Small Outfit Make a Big Impact?" and one of his points was "by lasting longer." Lorne said that our goal is to *finish well*. To be significant we must stay in the race. This means we have to be stern masters of our bodies. Pampering our bodily appetites is a sure way to become disqualified. One's body is unruly and difficult to manage. It doesn't want to get up, or pray, or leave a comfortable home for the battle line. Winning is done in the last lap of the race, the last quarter of the game, by one who has endurance. And endurance comes through relentless training—the kind of training which comes from regularly getting enough rest, eating moderately, and exercising. The late "Bear" Bryant, winning Alabama football coach, said that in order to play tough on Saturday, you had to live tough all week. "But I pommel my body and subdue it, lest after preaching to others, I myself should be disqualified" (1 Cor. 9:27, RSV). Lorne finished, "Let's determine to be those who last, to be in there strong for a good last lap, a great fourth quarter."

Pace

Some people never learn to pace themselves. They burn the candles of their lives at both ends, going 100 miles an hour until they either collapse, become ill, or are forced to rest. The young missionary McCheyne lived only 29 years and said just before he died, "God has given me a message to deliver and a horse to ride. I have killed the horse and now can no longer deliver the message." God continually renews His challenge to me to keep in as good shape physically as possible, because lack of physical well-being spills over to mental, emotional, and even spiritual areas which Satan would like to hurt and destroy.

One minister told of a period in his life when he began to react to situations far differently than usual. He became irritable, distracted, and extremely emotional. He felt it was an attack of Satan on his life. One morning at breakfast he burst into tears for no reason at all. This incident forced him to go for counsel to a godly, older minister who was also a good friend.

When the distraught man walked into the office of his friend, he said, "I need help. I feel that I am under a terrible attack of Satan."

The older man took one look at the young pastor and said, "Attack of Satan nothing. You get yourself to a hospital!"

As it turned out, the younger minister spent three months in a hospital recovering from a severe blood deficiency.

When we begin to experience unusual emotional symptoms, one of the first things we should do is to have a thorough physical examination. Our physical well-being, or lack of well-being, affects our emotional, mental, and spiritual health. Satan will take advantage of any weak area in our lives and try to hinder what God wants to do in and through our lives.

Goals

At age 50, I made some goals for myself. One of them was to climb Pikes Peak. I trained hard for it. With much effort, I worked out every day, especially doing exercises that helped my weak knee. The training to make it up Pikes Peak with several friends was solely my responsibility. What an encouragement and thrill it was to reach the top after seven and a half hours—weary, but victorious! I had accomplished that goal by training for it.

At the same time I determined to climb the Peak, I also had a goal to study the subject of godliness in Scripture, which I am still doing. No one is forcing me to do this. No professor is looking over my shoulder. I have committed myself and *I* have to do it.

So a primary thing that struck me in my new life passage

is that the responsibility for training in godliness is mine alone. God is definitely involved in this training, but the obligation to do it is mine. I am convinced there is no area of life that godly character doesn't touch in some way—whether it is ministry, relationships, thought-life, or attitudes. It is godliness (God-in-us) of character that prevents that "second look" at temptation which causes one to fall. It is godliness that responds with patience to one who is angry or ugly, or to a needle-stuck-on-the-same-depressing-record person. It is godliness that keeps looking for the possibilities rather than wallowing in the problems. It is godliness that is steadfast when the ball breaks a string on our life's racquet, that is loving when hit by an overhead smash, and that is kind when an obviously bad call has been made against us.

The value of training in godliness is not limited. It is valuable in *every way.* Physical fitness, Paul says, has *some* value, but godliness is of value in everything!

In addition to 1 Timothy 4:8, the Greek word for "training" is used three other times in the New Testament—only once with a negative connotation. That's when Peter described ungodly people who "have eyes full of adultery, insatiable for sin. They entice unsteady souls. They have hearts *trained* in greed" (2 Peter 2:14, RSV). The NIV says, "They are experts in greed." So it is possible to train ourselves in immoral characteristics as well as in godliness. In a sense, we are training ourselves in *something* all the time whether we like it or not. An indolent, not disciplined, personality is being "trained" in laziness. An unruly tongue let loose is being trained in maliciousness and anger. And then there are those who are deliberately training themselves in greed—money-grubbers—whose basic goal in life is to make more and more almighty dollars. Their lives are characterized by "insatiable sin" and they are experts in greed. We need to periodically examine ourselves to determine in what areas we are training ourselves.

Watch

Years ago I was challenged by Matthew 26:41: "Watch and pray so that you will not fall into temptation. The spirit is willing but the body is weak." I knew what it meant to pray, but what did it mean to "watch"? God began to show me that one of the things involved in "watching" is *knowing yourself* so that you can be on guard against areas of vulnerability and weakness. It means being acutely aware of how the enemy can get in to destroy what God wants to do in and through your life.

Recently a wife told us about her husband who is in full-time Christian work. Three or four times he had become emotionally involved with a woman who had come to him for counsel and help. Each time his family and his ministry were hurt. Yet he continued to counsel women without his wife being present.

That man failed to "watch." He refused to learn about himself, his emotional weakness, his area of vulnerability, and so failed to flee from repeated temptations.

I have a very competitive nature—which means I have to work in order to play competitive sports "just for fun." (My wife Carole is just the opposite—she really doesn't care how well she plays if it *is* fun!) Because I know myself in this area, I can take steps to "watch" myself—in some cases not playing at all. (I'd probably read the book *How to Win at Pac-Man* and practice until I *could* win if I ever let myself start playing that game.) At other times I take steps to not let a game consume me instead of using it as a recreational outlet.

We must be knowledgeable of ourselves. Do we have difficulty controlling the hours we watch television—or *what* we watch? Are we careless in the books and magazines we read, the movies we choose? Is it a temptation to us to read or watch things which appeal to our sensual nature instead of those that edify us? Do we tend to be workaholics and not be balanced in the areas of rest, recreation, and time with our families? Are we aware of the time of day when we are at our best, our worst, our most creative, our most dull? Do we use this knowledge to plan our activities and the use of our time?

How well do we know our strengths and weaknesses in order to guard against temptations? How often *do* we "watch" and pray for strength as well as wisdom to overcome our weaknesses?

The other two passages using the word "train" are found in Hebrews. First, Hebrews 5:12-14: "In fact, though by this time you ought to be teachers, you need someone to teach you the elementary truths of God's Word all over again. You need milk, not solid food! Anyone who lives on milk, being still an infant, is not acquainted with the teaching about righteousness. But solid food is for the mature, who by constant use have *trained themselves* to distinguish good from evil" (italics mine). The second passage of Scripture will be discussed in chapter 2.

Obey

When I saw what this was saying—*really saying*—God wrote it on my heart with indelible ink. The Scripture speaks here about training through obedience to the Word of God. But the incredible fact is that training or strenuous exercise is to be used not in getting to *know* the Bible, but in *using* the Word in our lives.

This is the key passage in all of Scripture as it relates to the maturity of the believer—and *knowledge* is not even mentioned! Those people knew a lot theologically, but they weren't using what they knew. They were unskilled in the *use* of the Word. Obviously, we must know the Word before we can use the Word—either in our own lives or with someone else. But the point in this key passage, as throughout the Bible, is that the emphasis is on use, doing, and obedience. This passage is saying that mature Christians are people who habitually *use* the Word of God—who have a sensitivity to God's Word in every area of their lives.

The process of habitually practicing or obeying what God tells us to do makes us sensitive to Him. When we are sensitive, God doesn't have to hit us over the head with a two-by-four to get our attention. We become aware of His very *whisper*.

David has always been some kind of hero to me! I have a long list of reasons and one of them has to do with his regard for God's Word. David wrote the longest chapter in the Bible (Ps. 119) and all but 4 of its 176 verses have something to say about God's Word. After David fell into temptation and sinned with Bathsheba, God sent Nathan the prophet to point out that sin. David's response was to fall on his face before God and confess his sin. He repented with all of his heart (2 Sam. 11—12).

Saul, on the other hand, when confronted with his sin of disobeying God's command to destroy all the spoil from a battle, began to make excuses and blamed the people for what was *his* reponsibility (1 Sam. 15).

The longer I live, the more convinced I become that the difference between a godly person and an ungodly one is not that one sins and one doesn't. Both are going to sin. But the godly person *admits* his sin, takes responsibility for it, and confesses it to God.

The psalmist David exulted, "Many, O Lord my God, are the wonders You have done. The things You planned for us no one can recount to You; were I to speak and tell of them, they would be too many to declare" (Ps. 40:5). I want to be aware not only of God's wonders, but of all the things He has planned for me. I want to have in my life a sensitivity to God's voice. I want Him to be able to get my attention with a whisper. But God will not even try to get my attention unless I intend to obey when He speaks. "If anyone chooses to do God's will, he will find out whether My teaching comes from God or whether I speak on My own," Christ said (John 7:17).

Oswald Chambers put it this way: "The golden rule of understanding spiritually is not intellect, but obedience. If a man wants scientific knowledge, intellectual curiosity is his guide; but if he wants insight into what Jesus Christ teaches, he can only get it by obedience. If things are dark to me, then I may be sure there is something I will not do. Intellectual darkness comes through ignorance: spiritual darkness comes because of something I do not intend to obey."*

Our intention not to obey is sin and we are warned, "If I had cherished sin in my heart, the Lord would not have listened" (Ps. 66:18). The implication stands that He may not have spoken either. God tells us, "If you had responded to My rebuke, I would have poured out My heart to you and made My thoughts known to you" (Prov. 1:23).

Developing the habit of sensitivity to God's voice results in growth, maturity, and discernment—a discernment of that which is good and that which is bad—the ability "to distinguish good from evil" (Heb. 5:14).

The other night Carole and I were talking about growth— wanting to understand what indicated whether growth was or was not taking place in our lives. We were concerned that there might be a time when we thought we were changing or grow- ing, but might be deluding ourselves.

Carole asked, "How do we know when we are not really open to God's voice? How do we know when we are closed to some lesson God is trying to teach us?" After interacting awhile, we decided that if two or three believers who know and love us should point out the same thing in our lives and we mentally reject it, then we may well be closed to the voice of God. God undoubtedly uses those who know and love us to tell us things we need to know.

The Lord Jesus is our *best* Friend. He loves us beyond all

---

*Oswald Chambers, *My Utmost for His Highest*. Reprinted by permission of Dodd, Mead & Company, Inc.

others. And He wants to speak to us through His Word. When He speaks over and over and we don't pay attention, we stop growing.

So of primary importance in training ourselves in godliness is understanding the constant process of being trained through obedience to the Lord—of *using* the Word in our lives.

②
Train
for Endurance

C.S. Lewis wrote, "God whispers in our pleasure but shouts in our pain." In a unique way, God captures our attention through trouble, trials, and tears. God's writer put it, "No discipline seems pleasant at the time, but painful. Later on, however, it produces a harvest of righteousness and peace for those who have been *trained* by it" (Heb. 12:11). This verse is the second time the word "trained" is used in the Book of Hebrews, and the third time in our study.

Discipline

We are trained by God's discipline in our lives. That is, we are if we are God's own children—if He is our Father not by creation alone, but by adoption into His family.

I was almost 13 when I discovered my need to be one of God's adopted sons. The circumstances were a bit strange, but God will use any circumstance to make someone aware of his need for Him.

I was having a fight with David. That wasn't unusual. David, the minister's son, and I were frequently fighting. I had red hair and David had a temper too, so even though we were good friends, fists flew often.

In the middle of one fight (when I was winning), I heard a shout, "Stop that!" obviously coming from a male adult. We halted with fists in mid-air. Dr. Lindsey, David's father and a big man, stood on the porch. He said, "Come into my study, Jack." I thought, "Oh boy, I'm in for it now."

I squirmed in the big leather chair. But instead of a verbal tongue-lashing about fighting with his son, Dr. Lindsey began to talk with me about my relationship with God. He reminded me that all of us are sinners. (I couldn't deny that right then!) He said that we have all fallen short of the holiness of God and told me that the payment for that guilt was death—separation from God Himself. In Romans 6:23 we read, "The wages of sin is death." But he also pointed out the verse doesn't stop there—that "the gift of God is eternal life through Jesus Christ our Lord."

He told me that God requires righteousness in order to enter heaven to be with Him. People, from Adam on, have rebelled against God and have gone their own way. But even if they try their very best, they can't begin to live up to the holiness which God requires. In His *justice,* God demands payment for our sin.

But because He loves us so much, He Himself, in the person of His Son Jesus, paid that penalty which was death. Christ met all of God's requirements for righteousness. He never sinned, never had cause for separation from His Father. After living a perfect life to teach us about the Father, He could have gone back to live with Him again without ever suffering separation, pain, and death.

Instead, Jesus chose to pay the terrible price of death on a cruel cross. He who knew no sin *became* sin and this broke His heart. He chose to die that, in accepting His sacrifice in my place, I might live forever. And then He proved that He was who He said He was, God Himself, by rising from the dead.

After Dr. Lindsey had finished, he turned to me and asked a question no one had asked me before. "Jack, have you ever received Jesus Christ into your life?"

When I replied that I hadn't, he said, "Would you like to right now?"

I said, "Yes, Sir, I would," and we knelt together, my face buried in that old leather chair. I asked Christ into my life. At that moment, I became an adopted son of God—one of His forever.

God trains His *children.* He is faithful to do so as a kind Father, a perfect Father. And one of the ways He trains us is by His discipline.

Discipline is painful. And I hate pain of any kind.

It is inevitable that we all have been, are right now, or will in the future face some hard, painful experiences. What will be our response? Will we look to Jesus and say, "Yes, I really do believe in the sovereignty of God; He is in control and I want to be open to what He is teaching me through this"? Will we *endure?*

We all face major difficulties—deaths, illnesses, financial losses. But sometimes it's not the big things, but the irritations of life which can be most difficult to endure.

Last fall, for four and a half months, our daughter and her husband in Mexico went through "the saga of a VW van." They had purchased a 1978 VW van before leaving to minister in Mexico because they were told that VWs are made in Mexico and fixing it would be no trouble. What they didn't know was that the van they purchased had an oversized American engine in it!

In August while they were in Mexico City, four hours from their home in Guanajuato, the van conked out. The next four and one-half months were like an "As the World Turns" soap opera, featuring the harassing problems of a VW van filmed in living color and stereophonic sound. Parts that had to be brought from the States after weeks of hassle were either not the problem, were defective, or didn't work. One thing and another were tried, resulting in spending over $1,000, many days, trips back and forth on plane and bus to Mexico City, and no trans-portation for the whole time that wasn't borrowed, begged, or rented. This took place right in the middle of getting a new ministry started, relatives visiting, having a new baby, and taking their three-year-old son to preschool each morning.

But they endured.

No "reason" has been given by the Lord. Yet right at the end of this trial as Lynn was crying in her heart, "Lord, why have we had to spend all this money on our van—we could have given the money to the poor?", the Lord brought to her mind the incident when the disciples asked that same question con-cerning a woman who had broken her expensive perfume over the head of the Lord Jesus. And His answer to the disciples was His answer to Lynn. He said, "She has done a beautiful thing to Me. The poor you will always have with you, and you can help them any time you want. But you will not always have Me. She did what she could" (Mark 14:6-8). It was as though God was telling Lynn, "Look, your sacrifice of time and money are to Me a beautiful thing. Let Me decide how they are to be used. Trust Me." And she rested in that. They endured.

Reproof

"The ear that heareth the reproof of life abideth among the wise. He that refuseth instruction despiseth his own soul; but he that heareth reproof getteth understanding" (Prov. 15:31-32).

Almost weekly we experience some reproof of life. How we handle it—what we do with it—how we look at such reproof—is vital. The reproof may be a great big thing that slaps us on the side of life like a 10-ton truck, or a small thing that God wants to use to teach us patience and understanding. The key is, How do we view it? How are we handling it? "When trouble comes, the really decisive question is not what happens *to* us, but what happens *in* us" (Oswald Chambers).

There are at least three ways we can respond to the reproofs of life.

Stoicism

First, we can respond stoically. We can grit our teeth and say, "I *will* get through this" and tough it out. But what is the result of this kind of response? Nothing. Absolutely nothing. We won't learn a single thing from the painful situation and no one else will learn from it either.

Some people say they have had 10 years' experience. But a stoic response—an inability to allow God to teach through the experience—means that those people did not gain 10 years' experience. They have had 1 year's experience repeated 10 times—and haven't even learned from that 1 year.

Bitterness

A second way of responding is with bitterness. Bitterness is the result of imagined or real ill treatment. Instead of viewing that treatment as "a reproof of life"—as a part of God's training program for us—resentment and bitterness are allowed to grip one's heart.

There are many ways to identify a bitter spirit, but I'd like to suggest just three:

(a) Bitterness is characterized by an unforgiving spirit. Paul wrote: "Get rid of all bitterness, rage, and anger, brawling and slander, along with every form of malice. Be kind and compassionate to one another, forgiving each other, just as in Christ God forgave you" (Eph. 4:31-32). A companion passage is 2 Corinthians 2:9-11: "The reason I wrote you was to see if you would stand the test and be obedient in everything. If you forgive anyone, I also forgive him. And what I have forgiven—if there was anything to forgive—I have forgiven in the sight of Christ for your sake, in order that Satan might not outwit us. For we are not unaware of his schemes."

Forgiveness is a preventive measure to keep Satan from gaining advantage in our midst. But bitterness is one of Satan's best tools and he tries to use it on all of us.

Years ago a young man lived in our home for several months when I sensed there was something wrong. One night as we were sitting in the living room, I began to ask him what was the matter. I said, "Buddy, you seem very unhappy. You act rather uptight with me. Is there something wrong between us?"

It took a bit of asking, but finally I got the pump primed and it really began to pour out. He was bitter against both Carole and me.

In several areas he mentioned, I had been wrong and I apologized. I asked his forgiveness and he said he forgave me.

A few days went by and some other things came up and I asked him about them. After we had talked I asked, "Is there anything else I need to know?"

"No, there is nothing more," he replied.

But it was obvious that there was. Several other times I asked him. At his wedding, still feeling as though there was something between us, I asked him once more. He was all smiles and said that all was well. But it wasn't. He was a bitter man.

Shortly after he got married, he forbade his wife to have anything to do with us. He cut off all relationships with his old friends in The Navigators. And over the years we heard he was going downhill spiritually. A few months ago, we heard that he had divorced his wife, leaving his son as well. Inside, we wept.

If not dealt with, a "root of bitterness" (Heb. 12:15, KJV) will grow until it brings devastating consequences to our lives, and it will always affect others around us.

During this time, I had occasion to ask Lorne Sanny what I

could do to help this fellow. Lorne looked sad as he said, "Jack, I wish I knew. I've known many men who over the years have turned bitter. Once that bitterness has gotten so far, there seems to be little hope. Very few turn back."

So what is our answer? It is found in Hebrews 12:14 which says: "Make every effort to live in peace with all men and to be holy; without holiness no one will see the Lord." Make every effort—strive—to pursue peace. This is a strong word in the Greek. It is the same word as in 2 Timothy 2:22 where we're told to "*pursue* righteousness, faith, love, and peace." It means to bend every effort, to get at it, not to let it escape you. In Philippians 3:14 the same Greek word is translated *"press on,"* toward the goal.

I have to *pursue* peace with people. To pursue peace and to be bitter at the same time are impossible. They cannot coexist. Paul made it clear: "So I strive always to keep my conscience clear before God and man" (Acts 24:16). I must pursue peace both manward and Godward. If I pursue peace with people and sanctification with God, I cannot be bitter. But this is *my* responsibility. I must keep short accounts with both the Lord and others or bitterness can grow into a terrible fire-breathing dragon that destroys everything in its path.

(b) Another sign of a bitter spirit is the habitual verbalizing to others about some ill treatment received—whether it is real or imagined. As Jesus said, "Out of the abundance of the heart, the mouth speaks" (Matt. 12:34, RSV). If we find ourselves frequently in mental conversations telling the person who mistreated us what we *really* think, or if we relive the event over and over in our minds, then we are bitter. God's Word says that our bitterness is going to cause trouble. It is going to hurt and defile many (Heb. 12:15).

To be "defiled" means to "tinge, stain, dye with another color, pollute, contaminate, soil" (W.E. Vine). In this passage, the word "defile" means moral defilement.

How do we defile someone? We talk about him! The whole ugly situation spills over into numerous conversations. Sometimes we tell people about problems we have with persons or organizations under the guise of asking for prayer. Our emotion-packed words, the inflections of our voices, the expressions on our faces tinge the thinking of those listening. We are literally "dyeing" the situation with another color, poisoning others' thoughts, and by so doing, we defile.

This defilement can be subtle as it probably was with Absalom when he went around the country undermining his father David until he "stole the hearts of the men of Israel" (2 Sam. 15:6). Or it can be as blatant as Shimei who cursed David and threw stones and dust at him (2 Sam. 16:5-14).

(c) The third characteristic of a bitter heart is a refusal to admit one's bitterness and thus learn the lessons that God intended by allowing that situation. Bitterness is one of the most difficult sins to admit. Many refuse to call it by name.

At times only God and you are aware of the temptation to be bitter. The battle is fought, won, or lost in your own heart alone. At other times the situation is blackened with soot and hung out on display in full view of the world. And the world awaits to see what we will do with our dirty laundry.

In either case, the danger is great because our hearts are deceitful and desperately wicked (Jer. 17:9 KJV); one's own heart can fool even the most honest person. I have seen people put on big smiles and tell me everything was fine when they were totally bitter inside. Their actions showed it, others could see it, but they were really blind to it. They might say, "I'm deeply hurt," or "I'm really frustrated," or "I'm greatly depressed about this thing" instead of admitting their resentment. We can have these other emotions without bitterness, of course. But we need to let God examine our hearts deeply to be sure that the root-cause of our hurt, frustration, or depression is not the anger of bitterness. We need to face up to any root of bitterness immediately and deal with it. We cannot afford to let it grow to contaminate our lives and the lives of those around us.

How can you know if your heart is deceiving you? If two or three of your best friends ask you if (or tell you!) you are bitter, you need to do some honest probing as to what they have observed to ask that. Then you need to spend some extended time before God, in the light of Psalm 139:23-24—"Search me O God, and know my heart; test me and know my anxious thoughts. See if there be any offensive way in me, and lead me in the way everlasting"—with an open heart, open Bible, and open notebook. Then let the searchlight of God's Word and Spirit enlighten your heart. If you have a godly mate, counselor, or friend, you need to ask that person for an honest evaluation. And finally you need to say, "Lord, if I've missed finding even the smallest root of bitterness in my heart, please probe deeply and bring to bear anything needed, to make me see what it is and call it by its name."

If you find any bitterness at all caused by real or supposed ill-treatment—or anything else for that matter—you have only one option before God. And that is, to forgive.

Charles Swindoll, in his book *Improving Your Serve,* has a profound thought about the meaning of Matthew 18:34. This is the ending sentence of the story Christ told about the kingdom of heaven being compared to a certain king who wished to settle accounts with his slave. The king forgave the huge debts which the slave owed him, but the forgiven slave turned around and would not forgive a fellow slave who owed him only a small amount. The account ends with the verse, "And his lord, moved with anger [over the unforgiving spirit of the slave he had absolved of debt], handed him over to the torturers until he should repay all that was owed him" (NASB).

Mr. Swindoll suggests that this slave's torture was an inner torment. He says, "... the one who refuses to forgive, the

Christian who harbors grudges, bitter feelings toward another, will be turned over to torturous thoughts, feelings of misery, and agonizing unrest within."

Ray Stedman, in a sermon, described it like this: "This is a marvelously expressive phrase to describe what happens to us when we do not forgive another. It is an accurate description of gnawing resentment and bitterness, the awful gall of hate or envy. It is a terrible feeling. We cannot get away from it. We feel strongly this separation from another and every time we think of that person we feel within the acid of resentment and hate eating away at our peace and calmness. This is the torturing that our Lord says will take place."

Acceptance

The third and right way to respond to the reproofs of life is by lifting our hearts to God and saying, "Lord, this is tough. It is hard to go through. But I know You are permitting this. So don't allow me to miss out on any of the things You want to teach me." God wants us to respond with open hearts to Him and when we do, it yields "the peaceable fruit of righteousness" (Heb. 12:11, KJV) in our lives. The result of responding rightly will be peace. People around us will be strengthened and blessed and there will be "a harvest of righteousness" (12:11, NIV).

Training in godliness is a process—one that will last for the rest of my life. My friend who ran the marathon said, "In the Christian life, the training we get daily at the feet of Jesus is the key to performance. We may share the Gospel for 30 minutes with a non-Christian, but behind that witness must be a life filled and prepared by the Holy Spirit over months of faithfulness."

God is greatly interested in that process. So often we are anxious to "get there"—to be godly—to finish the race. But God is as interested in the process as He is in the end product. Oswald Chambers put it this way:

We are apt to imagine that if Jesus Christ constrains us, and we obey Him, He will lead us to great success. We must never put our dreams of success as God's purpose for us: His purpose may be exactly the opposite. We have an idea that God is leading us to a particular end, a desired goal; He is not. The question of getting to a particular end is a mere incident. What we call the process, God calls the end.

What is my dream of God's purpose? His purpose is that I depend on Him and His power now. If I can stay in the middle of the turmoil calm and unperplexed, that is the end of the purpose of God. God is not working towards a particular finish; His end is the process—that I see Him walking on the waves, no shore in sight, no success, no goal, just the absolute certainty that it is all right because I see Him walking on the sea. It is the process, not the end, which is glorifying to God.

God's training is for now, not presently. His purpose is for this minute, not for something in the future. We have nothing to do with the afterwards of obedience; we get wrong when we think of the afterwards. What men call training and preparation, God calls the end.

God's end is to enable me to see that He can walk on the chaos of my life just now. If we have a further end in view, we do not pay sufficient attention to the immediate present; if we realize that obedience is the end, then each moment as it comes is precious.*

Training myself in godliness is for now. It is present tense. If I'm not involved in that training *today,* I have missed out not only in a day of vital training, but in a day of "process" which to God *is* the goal.

---

*Oswald Chambers, *My Utmost for His Highest* (Dodd, Mead & Company), pp. 209–10.

3

Build Yourself
in the Word (Part 1)

It has been said, "You don't *think* your way to faith, you *obey* your way to faith." When I am willing to obey—to step out on the promises of God even if I am scared to death—I find He is faithful and my confidence in my faithful God begins to grow. But it takes going forth, acting on, and obeying God's commands even when my faith is small. One of the secrets of success in the Christian life is putting the Scriptures to use.

Use

In a thundering command to Joshua, the Lord God Himself said, "Do not let this Book of the Law depart from your mouth; meditate on it day and night, so that you may be careful to do everything written in it. Then you will be prosperous and successful" (Josh. 1:8).

Christ reinforced these words when He said, "Whoever has My commands and obeys them, he is the one who loves Me. He who loves Me will be loved by My Father, and I too will love him and show Myself to him" (John 14:21).

Do you have a sense of Jesus Christ showing or manifesting

Himself to you daily? Is He becoming more real and are you learning new things about Him each week? As you look back one year, is He more of a Companion and Friend this year than He was a year ago? This promise—that He will show Himself to you—is contingent on your *obeying* His Word.

Jesus told a story of two men consumed with the same task—that of building a house. He said:

> Therefore everyone who hears these words of Mine and puts them into practice is like a wise man who built his house on the rock. The rain came down, the streams rose, and the winds blew and beat against that house; yet it did not fall, because it had its foundation on the rock.

> But everyone who hears these words of Mine and does not put them into practice is like a foolish man who built his house on sand. The rain came down, the streams rose, and the winds blew and beat against that house, and it fell with a great crash (Matt. 7:24-27).

One man built his spiritual life on the true foundation—Jesus Christ—and on a day-by-day use of the Scriptures. He heard God's words and put them into practice. The other man built on sand. He read, heard, and went about his own business, doing what he pleased. He did not put God's words into practice. The first man built his life on obedience to the Scripture. The other man built his life on expediency and personal desires. Then the floods of life came—the trials and the storms. The man whose house was built on the rock withstood the storms because his life was based on the solid foundation of the Word of God. But the man who had built his life on the expedient thing—the thing that was best for *him,* his own personal desires—found that when the floods came in, the foundation on which his life had been built washed away.

The Lord's desire for us is found in Isaiah 66:1-2: " 'Heaven is My throne and the earth is My footstool. Where is the house you will build for Me? Where will My resting place be? Has not My hand made all these things, and so they came into being?' declares the Lord. 'This is the one I esteem: he who is humble and contrite in spirit, and trembles at My Word.' "

Do we *tremble* at the Word of God? I don't mean with *fear* —but in the realization of who God is and out of respect, awe, and love for Him? Practical obedience should be a part of everything in our lives. "Your hearts must be fully committed to the Lord our God, to live by His decrees and obey His commands" (1 Kings 8:61). This is our command and should be our experience. God is looking for people "whose hearts are fully committed to Him" (2 Chron. 16:9). A committed heart is a heart that is yielded in obedience to His Word—a person who keeps God's commandments day after day—who *listens* and then acts. One with a committed heart hears, ponders, meditates, chews it over, digests it, and then *does* what God lays on his heart to do.

We are to obey God's Word and then we use it as the sword of the Spirit, because that is exactly what it is! (Eph. 6:17)

Tom, one of the men in a Bible study, was trying to witness to a fellow worker who didn't believe the Bible. He asked the others, "What do you do when you have a friend you are talking to about the Lord and you use the Scriptures but the friend says, 'Don't preach the Bible to me. I don't believe it'?"

After they talked about Tom's problem for a few minutes, they decided that perhaps he should lay off using the Bible for a while and then let it creep back into the conversation later.

Then we looked at Ephesians 6:17 which says, "Take the helmet of salvation and the sword of the Spirit, which is the Word of God." I pointed out to the men that the Word of God is the *sword* of the Spirit. It is a discerner of the thoughts and intents of the heart (Heb. 4:12). I asked, "Supposing I had a gun in my hand—a loaded .45 automatic—and I held it to your head. You smiled at me with a silly grin on your face and said, 'Well, I don't believe in guns' and I pulled the trigger. What would happen?"

One man replied, "Boom!" and everyone laughed.

I continued, "Yes, it would blow a pretty good-size hole in your head. It wouldn't matter at all whether you believed in guns or not."

We talked then about the fact that God's Word *is* a sword. You don't have to defend a sword. You just use it. They got the point!

But remember, Friend, it is a sword, not a club. There is a difference in the way one uses a sword and a club. We need to wield the sword with skill and finesse. It takes experience and time to develop such proficiency. Anyone can go mauling around a crowd with a club, but it usually doesn't accomplish as much as a sword. We need to use the Scriptures as our authority in an expert manner.

Authority

For us to be motivated to use the Scriptures, we must be convinced first of all of their authority—an authority which comes from God Himself.

If you came to Colorado Springs and began to speed along Academy Boulevard, going 50 mph in a 35 mph zone, I might pull up beside you and yell, "Hey, Buddy, you are going 15 mph over the speed limit."

Probably you would respond, "So what?"

But if a police officer pulled up beside you and said, "Hey, Buddy, you are going 15 mph over the speed limit," you would say, "Oh, I'm sorry, Sir!"

The source determines authority. In that situation I don't have any authority to back up my words, but the police officer does.

God Himself is the Source of the Scriptures and He gives His Word absolute authority. Webster defines authority as "that which is entitled to obedience" or "that property by which it demands faith and obedience in all its declarations." I like that.

Authority means it is not for me to decide what to believe or obey. If I believe in the authority of the Scriptures, I believe it all.

Someone has said, "What is in the Bible is not true only because it is in the Bible. It was true before it was in the Bible. It is in the Bible because it is true." Jesus declared, "Your [God's] Word is truth" (John 17:17).

What then should be our response to the authority of the Scriptures?

We need to accept them by faith.

Before Billy Graham became a world-renowned evangelist, he had some real conflicts in his own mind concerning the Bible. He wrestled with his questions and doubts. Finally he went out in the woods, placed his Bible on a tree stump, got down on his knees, and cried out before the Lord, "I believe all of this is Your Word. From this point on I will never question its authority again." It is recorded in his biography that it was from this point in time that God really began to pour out His Spirit on this man and use him in a tremendous way.

In order for God to use the Scriptures through us, we must come to that place where by faith we no longer question the authority of the Bible. We will never be able to resolve all the intellectual questions or problems that men have debated for centuries, but by faith we have settled forever that the Bible is the Word of God and therefore absolutely true.

Value

The source of the authority of the Bible is God Himself. Therefore, it cannot help but have great value in our lives, if we learn it and live by it.

I once did a study on the ministry of the Word to me as a believer—what it does in my life as a Christian. And what the Word does for me is absolutely fantastic!

The Bible strengthens me and develops my faith. It cleanses me and aids me to have victory over sin. It guides me, searches the motives of my heart, brings joy, and produces peace.* And this is just a partial list of all the Word does for me!

"All Scripture is God-breathed and is useful for teaching, rebuking, correcting, and training in righteousness, so that the man of God may be thoroughly equipped for every good work" (2 Tim. 3:16-17).

The Bible is *God-breathed!* He has spoken and is to be taken seriously. This passage tells us that it is profitable—useful—in four different ways:

1. For teaching or doctrine. Webster defines doctrine as a "principle or position in a system of belief acceptable as authoritative." In other words, the Word of God teaches us what we should know about God Himself, about people, sin, heaven, hell, and life.

2. For reproof or rebuking. Reproof is defined as "censure for a fault." The Bible teaches us what we should stop doing.

3. Correction. This is defined as "bringing into conformity with a standard or something substituted in place of what is wrong." In other words, the Bible teaches us what we should start doing.

4. Instruction or training in righteousness. This speaks of living a Christlike life, or practical righteousness. Paul wrote, "It is because of Him [God] that you are in Christ Jesus, who has become for us wisdom from God—that is, our righteousness, holiness, and redemption" (1 Cor. 1:30). It is through Jesus Christ's righteousness that we are righteous. It is through

---

*See Acts 20:32; Romans 10:17; John 15:3; Psalm 119:11, 105, 165; Hebrews 4:12; Jeremiah 15:16.

the Scripture that He instructs us in righteous living. The Bible teaches us what we should continue to do.

I like to think of it this way: We are walking along a boardwalk (the doctrine or teaching of the Word) and we veer off and fall into the mud. God's Word reproves us and says, "Don't do that." Then it says, "This is how to get back on the walk"—that's correction. Finally it teaches us how we can continue to stay on the boardwalk, which is instruction in righteousness.

The end result is so "the man of God may be thoroughly equipped for every good work" (2 Tim. 3:17). Who is a person of God? He is one who is "wise for salvation through faith in Christ Jesus" (v. 15). Such a person has available to him the inspired Scriptures which help him become mature and complete. Notice that it says "*may* be thoroughly equipped." It doesn't say every Christian *will* be. It all depends on us and our heart-attitudes toward the Scripture. If I *determine* to "build myself in the most holy faith and keep myself in God's love" (Jude 21) by applying my heart to the Word of God, then I will become mature, equipped. Equipped for what? "For *every* good work." Do you really suppose it means *"every"?* All? Might it not mean "certain kinds of good works"? After all, we don't all have great ability or talent. But it says "every," doesn't it?

I would define a "good work" here in a broad sense to mean anything that God would ask me to do. This passage is saying that the Scriptures are profitable to you and me in order to equip us to do *anything* God asks us to do! Think about that! It isn't a college education that equips us—not even a seminary degree can do that. We are equipped through the Word of God.

Bob Boardman came to know Christ during World War II out in the South Pacific. While there he was shot through the throat by a sniper's bullet, which forced him to talk in a husky whisper from then on.

When the war was over and he got out of the Marines, Bob spent a year at Biola, a Christian Bible School, and then was asked by Dawson Trotman to come and live in his home. All the men who lived with Dawson and Lila had certain jobs and responsibilities around the home or office of the fledgling organization of The Navigators.

Bob's assignment was the yard—a full-time job as it was a very large yard. Bob felt God was calling him to the mission field and struggled over how he could prepare for this by the kind of work he did in the yard. One day he was reviewing 2 Timothy 3:16-17 and was challenged by the fact that the Word of God was all he needed to do anything God asked him to do. Boardy got down on his knees before the Lord and claimed that promise from God. He began to work diligently to saturate his life with the Word. He had a lot of time by himself as a gardener working in the yard, cutting grass, trimming hedges, and planting flowers. During the two or three years he worked in that huge yard, he figured out all sorts of ways to meditate and memorize Scripture, such as putting verses around his watchband. As the lawns soaked in the water, Bob soaked in the Word. In the evenings he ministered to men, putting into practice what God was teaching.

One day Daws asked Bob to pray about going to Japan and ministering. Because Bob had been shot by the Japanese in Okinawa, he struggled with this decision. But he eventually responded to God's specific call. When he went to Japan, the Lord gave him a deep, heartfelt love for the Japanese. Bob and his wife Jean diligently studied the language and began a ministry among the Japanese people.

After one term in Japan, and a time in Okinawa, Bob and his family were on furlough in the States when he applied for a visa to return. Much to his surprise, his application was rejected. Boardy went to see the Japanese Consul to ask why his application had been turned down. Bob said, "We have been out in

Japan for six years now. Why is our visa application being denied?"

The consul replied, "You are a missionary, aren't you, Mr. Boardman?"

"Yes," Bob acknowledged.

"We have checked your credentials carefully and as far as we can tell, you have no qualifications whatever to be a missionary."

"What do you mean?" Bob asked.

"You have one year at a Bible college and you have not been ordained. Is that true?"

Bob said it was.

"Then why should we let you go back as a missionary?" the consul asked.

Bob pondered a moment and then inquired, "What if I get ordained? Will that help?"

"Yes, we will reconsider if you get ordained," was the response.

So a group of 16 pastors was formed as an ordination council to examine Bob on his qualifications to be in the Christian ministry. The pastors did not know Bob so one of the first questions they asked was what education Bob had. Bob said, "Well, one year at Oregon State College. And then I had one year at the Bible Institute of Los Angeles."

"What else?"

"That's all."

Of course, that news really made the pastors sit up straight! And they began to thoroughly question Bob as to his qualifications for the ministry. They asked him deep theological questions to find out what he knew and believed on many subjects. After each question was asked, Bob took the Bible and went from passage to passage answering it.

Finally it got to the place where the pastors had to stop him before he finished because his answers were so long and complete. They would say, "Well, that's enough on that question. Let's go on to something else." After an hour or so, it became apparent to these men that Boardy was eminently qualified to be a missionary and to be ordained as a minister of the Gospel of Jesus Christ. One of the last questions was, "Mr. Boardman, would you please pick out a book of the Bible and give us an exegesis on it, an outline of the content and the thrust of the book?"

Bob asked, "Which book would you like me to take?"

They chuckled and said, "Any one you want."

So Bob took the Book of 2 Timothy which he had memorized and opened the truths to them. He told of what it meant to him personally and especially spoke of 2 Timothy 2:2 which says, "And the things you have heard me say in the presence of many witnesses entrust to reliable men who will also be qualified to teach others." He spoke of his vision and heart to multiply his life into the lives of people everywhere and how this vision was being worked out in Japan.

After Bob had been ordained, the chairman of the council wrote a letter to Lorne Sanny, president of The Navigators, complimenting him for having such an outstanding man on his staff. The letter said, "I have sat on many ordination councils but I have never examined a man who is more qualified than Mr. Boardman to be a minister of Jesus Christ. I compliment you on this man."

A number of years ago, I had the privilege of following Bob around Tokyo for three weeks. What a challenge! There was not a taxi driver that he did not witness to. I heard him give his testimony in his husky-whisper voice to a student Karate team and I was awed.

"That the man of God may be thoroughly equipped . . . "

Bob was equipped.

Lorne Sanny said some time ago, "While some people work at rewriting the Bible, we will use it to rewrite history—the history of individual lives."

And Dawson Trotman, who trained Bob Boardman, said, "All we want to do is to get every person in the world into the Bible." That's all! Daws really had that on his heart and it was why he developed simple tools and techniques of Bible study, Scripture memorization, and ways that emphasize the *how* of getting people into the Word of God and getting the Word into them.

> Great truths are greatly won. Not found by chance,
>   Nor wafted on the breath of summer dream,
> But grasped in the great struggle of the soul,
>   Hard buffeting with adverse wind and stream.
>
> Grasped in the day of conflict, fear, and grief,
>   When the strong hand of God, put forth in might,
> Plows up the subsoil of the stagnant heart,
>   And brings the imprisoned truth-seed to the light.
>
> Wrung from the troubled spirit in hard hours
>   Of weariness, solitude, perchance of pain,
> Truth springs, like harvest, from the well-plowed field,
>   And the soul feels it has not wept in vain.
>   —Horatius Bonar

4

Build Yourself in the Word (Part 2)

He stood against the backdrop of the massive granite fireplace in the Great Hall of Glen Eyrie, conference center of The Navigators. Short. Square-jawed. He spoke earnestly and his charisma provided a dynamic that dared us not to listen.

The year was 1956 and we were new to The Navigators organization, not yet having come on staff. We were more than a bit awed in the presence of its founder, Dawson Trotman. I will never forget his message that morning. He spoke on "The Qualifications of a Disciple" and his first point caused me much thought, for it was foundational to everything else he presented.

Devotional Life

A disciple, he said, must have a strong built-in devotional life. He must have a walk with Jesus Christ that is so stable it needs no propping up by others. It does not depend on "mountaintop experiences." Rather it is a steady walk, day after day after day.

I wonder how many Christians today have what could be

termed a strong, built-in devotional life. Many are characterized by the kind of Christianity that Chad Walsh talks about in his book, *Early Christians of the 21st Century.* He says, "Millions of Christians live in a sentimental haze of vague piety with soft organ music trembling in the lovely light from stained glass windows. Their religion is a pleasant thing of emotional quivers divorced from the will, divorced from the intellect, and demanding little except lip service to a few harmless platitudes. I suspect that Satan has called off his attempt to convert people to agnosticism. After all, if a man travels far enough away from Christianity he's liable to see it in perspective and decide that it is true. It is much safer from Satan's point of view to vaccinate a man with a mild case of Christianity so as to protect him from the real thing."

I am somewhat heartsick and appalled by the number of Christians I talk with concerning their standards of a walk with Jesus Christ. Many are satisfied with so little! Some are content with hearing the Word preached on Sunday mornings. Others are satisfied with a family devotional book read at a meal, or by studying a Sunday School lesson manual in preparation for a class. Many do not even have this intake of the Scriptures. These Christians are unaware they are starving to death spiritually. What they are experiencing isn't enough to provide sustenance in their walk with Jesus, let alone experience the power, strength, and victory that is needed to live the kind of life that gives impact for Christ.

When the 12 Apostles needed help in everyday affairs of the early church, they got together and chose seven men to look after the widows and orphans in their midst. The decision to pick these particular men was primarily based on what other people saw in their lives. They were men who had been observed to be full of the Spirit and wisdom. They had demonstrated in their lives certain qualities that exemplified a walk with Jesus Christ that was *built in* (Acts 6).

A walk like this does not happen overnight. A couple of verses tucked away in the Book of Jude challenge me constantly. They say, "But you, dear friends, build yourselves up in your most holy faith and pray in the Holy Spirit. Keep yourselves in God's love as you wait for the mercy of our Lord Jesus Christ to bring you to eternal life" (vv. 20-21).

Here are two imperatives which we are to *do ourselves:* (a) We are to build ourselves up in our most holy faith, and (b) we are to keep ourselves in God's love.

YBH?

A friend of mine tells the story of a man who borrowed a book from an acquaintance and was intrigued to find portions underlined with the letters YBH in the margin. When he returned the book, he asked the owner about the underlined sections with the YBH initials beside them. The owner replied, "Well, basically I agree with the paragraphs which are underlined. The YBH stands for, 'Yes, But How?' "

Yes, but how? Significant question. How do we build ourselves up in the faith? We do it by quality time, meaningful time, prayerful time in God's Word.

Mastery

Are we as Christians praying that God will give us an ever-growing mastery of the Bible? Are we praying for an ever-growing obedience to His Word in our daily lives? It has been said, "In order for the Master's life to master you, you must master the Master's life."

I had the privilege shortly after seminary to collaborate with Dr. Jack Mitchell—a man who is saturated in the Bible. Years ago we invited Dr. Jack to speak on the Book of Hebrews for two hours each day at a week-long staff conference. But Dr. Jack didn't speak on just Hebrews—he spoke on the whole *Bible* as he pulled one truth after another from the Scriptures to share with us. It was apparent that Dr. Jack was saturated with the Scriptures. The word "saturate" comes from the same base word in Latin, *satis,* as does the word "satisfy." *Satis* literally means "enough." The base *satur* in Latin means full of food, sated, to fill completely as if by soaking. If you take a sponge and soak it in water, it becomes so drenched that at the slightest squeeze, water comes out. That was the way it was with Dr. Jack. No matter where you poked him, the Bible came out!

Dr. Jack was raised in an Irish settlement in northeast England, close to the Scottish border. After migrating to Canada, he became a Christian while working as a tool-and-die maker. God gave him such a hunger for the Scriptures that each evening, after work, he would sit down at his desk and begin to read the Bible. In one drawer he kept big red apples. He would sit there at his desk, eating apples and soaking in the Scriptures. Many mornings his alarm clock would go off, telling him it was time to go to work and he would only then become aware that he had read all night.

When I attended seminary, Dr. Jack would come down from Portland every year to teach us two weeks of Bible. He would take the train so that he could have time to read the book he was teaching (no matter how many times he had taught it before) a minimum of 50 times! As a result, it was taught with a freshness of vision that stirred new life into the Word for us.

Another man immersed in the Word of God is Hubert Mitchell, a former missionary to Southeast Asia. Hubert's father returned to the mission field at age 80 and all of Hubert's children are in the ministry somewhere around the world. Hubert Mitchell once made this thought-provoking statement: "Of all the great Christians I've known, many started strong. But I have known few who *ended well."*

Dr. Jack Mitchell is one who has finished well. At the time of this writing, he is 90 and still preaching the Word of God strongly—and living it too.

Both Dr. Jack and Hubert Mitchell are challenges to me, not only because of their knowledge of the Scriptures, which is vast, but because of their observable application of God's Word to their daily lives.

"Yes, but how?" How do we build ourselves up in the Word of God? We must know it and live it.

Secondhand Knowledge

Most Christians' *knowledge* of the Word is secondhand. It has been gained by hearing sermons, listening to tapes, and reading books about the Bible. This is just secondhand knowledge, for someone else has done the study, the digging, the meditating, and the praying over the Word of God.

Don't misunderstand me. There is nothing wrong with hearing good sermons, listening to tapes, or reading books about the Bible. It is just not enough! We need more than that. We need personal and in-depth exposure to God's Word—firsthand knowledge as a result of our own effort.

Obedience

Most Christians' knowledge of the Word far exceeds their experience of *obedience* to the Word in daily life. They talk beyond their walk. These two aspects of building ourselves in the Word must be kept in balance.

Listen to what James, a half brother of the Lord, says about this concept: "Do not merely listen to the Word, and so deceive yourselves. Do what it says. Anyone who listens to the Word but does not do what it says is like a man who looks at his face in a mirror and, after looking at himself, goes away and immediately forgets what he looks like. But the man who looks intently into the perfect Law that gives freedom, and continues to do this, not forgetting what he has heard, but doing it—he will be blessed in what he does" (James 1:22-25).

Note that the emphasis is on "doing" rather than on "listening" (knowledge). However, we cannot do something we do not know about or have not heard about, so both knowledge and practice are important.

The "mirror" and the "perfect Law" have similar usefulness. A mirror reflects a perfect image of our physical features. The Word of God reveals a perfect image of our spiritual features. The admonition to us is to continually look intently into the Word of God and then put into practice what we see there.

"Yes, but how?"

A few weeks ago I was sitting in our family room, early in the morning having my quiet time. This has been a habit I have practiced for years—spending time each day alone with the living God to pray, read His Word, and meditate on it. I was praying that morning about a number of issues and people involved with my job. As I was praying, I began to realize that I was uptight concerning several things I was talking to God about. I was anxious. I was worried. As soon as I realized that, I also realized I was doing wrong. How did I know it was wrong? A passage of Scripture which I had memorized years ago hit me square in the heart: "Do not be anxious about anything, but in everything, by prayer and petition, with thanksgiving, present your requests to God. And the peace of God, which transcends all understanding, will guard your hearts and minds in Christ Jesus" (Phil. 4:6-7).

The application was obvious, but not easy. I confessed my worry as sin. Then I began to make specific requests of God regarding each issue. I thanked Him for His love and interest in these matters and for what He was going to do about them. As I did this, I began to experience an inner peace that God was in charge of my life.

What a way to start the day!

Just knowing the ideas, concepts, promises, and commands of Philippians 4:6-7 was not enough. Even having the verses memorized was not adequate. I had to apply these verses to a specific situation in my life in order for them to bear fruit. By the way, I had to repeat this process for about two weeks before I began to enjoy 24 consecutive hours of leaving those issues with God.

The Price

There is a price to pay in becoming saturated in God's Word. It takes a commitment to the Word that is lifelong. A commitment to become absorbed with God's Word.

One of the foundational blocks of building oneself up in God's Word is the practice I just mentioned—consistently spending some time with God. Every day. But one can even do this without meeting God. Many people have a habit of reading a chapter in the Bible and saying a prayer each day. But lots of them meet a *habit* rather than meeting *God.* And there is quite a difference.

We are told, "Let the word of Christ dwell in you richly" (Col. 3:16). If our daily devotional time only reaches the top of our minds, and does not consistently reach our hearts, we are not letting the Word of God dwell in us *richly.*

A simple plan to start letting the Word dig into your life is to pray for a hunger and thirst for God and for His Word and then approach your devotional time with a sense of expectancy—the expectancy of not just reading a book, but actually listening to a voice—God's voice.

Begin by praying Psalm 119:18: "Open my eyes that I may see wonderful things in Your Law." And then daily write down a wonderful thing that God shows you.

After you have prayed, read for four or five minutes from the Bible. Read slowly, meditatively, prayerfully. Then take two or three minutes to pray over what God has been speaking to you about.

Instead of trying to bite off 30 to 45 minutes and only doing it sporadically and then feeling guilty when you are inconsistent, begin to spend just 7 to 10 minutes of really quality time with the Saviour. But do it every day. This set-apart time each day will lead your heart back to the Lord throughout the day to pray for others and meditate on Him and His Word. It is not a "devotional life" but a life of devotion—a 24-hour walk with God—that is our goal. God will eventually give you a desire for the Word that will be so intense that the 10 minutes will not be enough and it will lengthen naturally.

I would suggest if you are just beginning to have a devotional time each day that you start by reading the Book of Mark, Philippians, or 1 Thessalonians before you begin to read the entire New Testament through. Then go back to the beginning—the Old Testament. But when you read the Old Testament, keep a finger in the Gospels so you can always keep the face of Jesus before you even as you read the God-inspired history, laws, and prophets of Israel. By that I mean, read a paragraph or so from a Gospel each day as well as your portion in the Old Testament.

Five Building Blocks

Other building blocks need to be placed in the "building of ourselves" in the Word. Other blocks in order to have a life which is saturated with the Scriptures are:

1. Hear the Word preached—I mean *really* hear without your mind being a million light years away. Take notes. Think about how to apply what you have heard. Write out the Scripture used, look it up, and check up on the accuracy of interpretation as the Bereans did: "Now the Bereans were of more noble character than the Thessalonians, for they received the message with great eagerness and examined the Scriptures every day to see if what Paul said was true" (Acts 17:11). If the Bereans could check up on the accuracy of Paul, I am sure your minister would not mind your checking up on him!

2. Read the Bible through in one or two years, perhaps with

a guide to accompany it. We can "skim" or we can "dwell richly." Have an underliner handy to use when the Spirit of God tells you to take note of something, along with a notebook to jot down ideas and thoughts. Ask God for concentration and understanding as you read.

3. Study the Bible with a group of people who challenge your thinking to dig deeper and deeper. Learn how to do inductive, chapter-by-chapter study which is the "meat and potatoes" of our diet in the Word.

4. Memorize passages and verses from the Bible. I can hear you saying, "But that's for kids! It's tough for adults to memorize. I'm too busy for that."

Through the years I have heard almost every excuse possible for not memorizing Scripture. So let me tell you something. *Don't memorize Scripture—unless,* of course, *you want God to change your life.* Because that is exactly what He will do if you hide His Word away in your heart. Someone has said, "I used to memorize Scripture, but now I learn it by heart." That is precisely what God wants you to do—to let His Word penetrate into the dailies of your life—to change your attitudes, thought patterns, habits, and character.

Any good translation is fine for memorizing. Usually using the same translation saves you from also remembering which Bible is used. (The Navigators Topical Memory System comes in four versions: the King James and the New International Versions on reversed sides, and the New American Standard and Revised Standard Versions on reversed sides.)

In 1956, as a youth director, I tried hard to get our young people to memorize Scripture. We had contests, prizes, all sorts of things to motivate them to memorize. But somehow, none were successful. I didn't see then, that the reason I was failing to inspire them, was because I didn't think it important enough for *me* to do.

Oh, I had started once in college. One day as I was standing in the dining hall line, I noticed a fellow nearby with a little leather packet in his hand. While waiting in line, this fellow would look at this packet, then look up at the sky. His lips would move a little bit. Then he would look down and repeat these strange maneuvers.

One day my curiosity got the better of me and I asked him what he was doing.

The mumbler responded, "I'm memorizing Scripture. I write down verses on these little cards and at spare moments, like standing in chow line, I go over them and review them." Then he began to put pressure on me, eventually poking me in the chest and saying, "Mayhall, you ought to be memorizing too."

Well, I was a Christian and I really couldn't argue with that. My acquaintance shoved three packets of verses—108 in all—into my hand and said, "Well, Mayhall, get started."

What motivation! What positive reinforcement! I memorized about six verses and then quit.

It wasn't until several years later that God showed me how necessary it is to hide His Word in my heart in order to absorb and be absorbed with the Word, so that at a moment's notice the Holy Spirit can speak to me through Scripture. Or through me, to someone else. This habitual practice began to change my life. I began to see bad attitudes change. Soon Carole noticed and wanted to know what was happening. This change in me made her want to begin memorizing Scripture too. Both of us say today that, for the time invested, Scripture memory has been the most effective intake of the Word into our lives for growth and change.

5. Meditate on the Word of God. Meditation is done with all of the first four methods of intake. When I listen, I can think about what I'm hearing and mentally apply the truths. When I read, I can chew on the message. When I study, I can mull over the depths to understand meanings. But in memorizing and in reviewing (which is the secret of effective memorization)

wherever I go, whatever I'm doing, at any moment when my mind is not actively involved in necessary thinking, I can review a verse I have memorized and meditate prayerfully on it.

Deliberate meditation is almost a lost art among us. Meditation is mental Bible study with a view to application. As we think about a verse, we can ask the "who, what, where, how, when" questions. "Who should do this? What does this really mean? What aspects are not in my life? Where should it be applied? How should I do this? When can I begin?"

Think about each word. Visualize the verse in application. Above all, ask God for wisdom to apply it. Then do it.

When we "dwell richly," we are constantly hearing, reading, studying, memorizing, and meditating with the thought in the back of our hearts, "How does God want me to apply what I am seeing?"

For years I didn't know how to take a Scripture passage out of the theoretical and put it into shoe-leather action. Then I discovered the tool of taking a verse I was memorizing or studying and writing it out in my own words: first writing how I had failed to live up to that verse, then writing down a specific illustration of my failure, and finally prayerfully letting God give me a plan to obey the truth of that verse within a week's period of time. Scripture began to become totally practical and took on a new meaning in my life.

We must be saturated, absorbed in God's Word. We must *dwell richly.*

"O the depths of the riches of the wisdom and knowledge of God! How unsearchable are His judgments, and His paths beyond tracing out!" (Rom. 11:33)

5

Build Yourself
in Prayer

Dr. D.E. Host, successor to J. Hudson Taylor of the China Inland Mission, was noted for being a man of great prayer. A young missionary who had heard of Dr. Host's reputation approached him after a meeting and asked, "Dr. Host, is there any possibility I could spend some time with you in prayer?"

Dr. Host answered, "By all means. Meet me in my room at 2:00 tomorrow afternoon and we will pray."

At 2:00 P.M. sharp the young man appeared at the hotel room. Dr. Host ushered him in and immediately said, "All right, let's pray." He got down on his knees and the young missionary knelt with him.

Dr. Host began to pray. He prayed. And he prayed. After about 30 minutes, the younger man thought he heard a different intonation, so he looked up and saw Dr. Host standing at the window looking out, but still praying. A few minutes later the missionary glanced up to see the director sitting in a chair still praying. For two hours Dr. Host prayed for people, cities, organizations, and ministries all around the world. Finally, he stopped.

There was a silence. The young missionary knew it was time for him to pray, but he couldn't figure out what there was left to pray for. After a moment, Dr. Host said it was his turn. The young man blurted, "I don't know what else there is to pray for, sir."

"Son," was Dr. Host's quiet response, "I have left you all of China."

The director of the China Inland Mission had left him "all of China."

Dr. Host had a friendship going—a friendship with Jesus Christ not based on academic knowledge but based on love, understanding, and confidence.

Converse

One of the primary ways we develop a friendship is by conversing. One definition of prayer is "a conversation between two people who love each other."

"Build yourselves up in your most holy faith and *pray* in the Holy Spirit. Keep yourselves in God's love" (Jude 20-21). One imperative for building ourselves—for keeping ourselves in God's love—is to *pray*. Prayer is the element which contributes the most to our falling in love with Jesus and sustaining that love as the years go by.

The great men of our Christian history were men of prayer. "God's acquaintance is not made hurriedly," wrote E.M. Bounds. "He does not bestow His gifts on the casual or hasty comer and goer. To be much alone with God is the secret of knowing Him and of influence with Him."

We read books, we hear sermons, we do studies on the subject of prayer. We know the Bible commands us to pray. Why is it then that many of us are so weak in the area of prayer? We have a legion of well-worn excuses ranging from "I don't know how" all the way to "I don't have time."

No time to pray!
O, why so fraught with earthly care
As not to give a humble prayer
   Some part of day?

No time to pray!
What heart so clean, so pure within,
That needeth not some check from sin,
   Needs not to pray?

No time to pray!
'Mid each day's dangers, what retreat
More needful than the mercy seat?
   Who need not pray?

No time to pray!
Must care or business' urgent call
So press us as to take it all,
   Each passing day?

What thought more dear
Than that our God His face should hide,
And say, through all life's swelling tide,
   No time to hear!
                —Anonymous

Understand and Know

Have you ever thought about what is uppermost on God's heart for you? Intriguing question, isn't it?

Listen to Jeremiah (9:23-24): "This is what the Lord says: 'Let not the wise man boast of his wisdom or the strong man boast of his strength or the rich man boast of his riches, but let him who boasts boast about this: that he *understands* and *knows* Me, that I am the Lord, who exercises kindness, justice, and righteousness on earth, for in these I delight,' declares the Lord" (author's italics).

Intellects with 130+ IQs should thank God for their brain-power, but should not brag about it. Atlas types—whether their strength is in physical power or in leadership or in position—should not be proud of God's gift to them. Wealth should not be flaunted. The *only* thing we may "boast about" is *understanding* and *knowing* God. (And really knowing Him will keep us humble!)

We are masters at getting involved in a crowded schedule of activities to the neglect of the truly important.

One day Christ dropped in for a visit on His friends Mary and Martha in Bethany. Not having telephoned ahead, Martha wasn't prepared for the visit and "was distracted by all the preparations that had to be made." In fact, Martha got quite angry at Mary for not helping her and finally in exasperation, she came to Christ and asked, "Lord, don't You care that my sister has left me to do the work by myself? Tell her to help me!"

The Lord's answer to her speaks to many of us—me included. He said, "Martha, Martha, you are worried and upset about many things, but only one thing is needed. Mary has chosen what is better, and it will not be taken away from her." Mary had chosen to sit "at the Lord's feet listening to what He said" (Luke 10:39-42).

On his deathbed, David told one of his sons, "As for you, my son Solomon, know the God of your father, and serve Him with a whole heart, and a willing mind; for the Lord searches all hearts, and understands every intent of the thoughts. If you seek Him, He will let you find Him; but if you forsake Him, He will reject you forever" (1 Chron. 28:9, NASB). Notice the order here. The *knowing* comes before the *serving* which is the order all through Scripture and is never reversed in the Bible. God's priority is always to first sit at the feet of Jesus. Only then are we equipped to serve Him.

If you were given an opportunity to stand up in front of a group and talk about Jesus Christ from the standpoint of your own personal relationship and experience with Him, how long could you talk? How much would you have to say about Him not only as your Saviour, but as your Friend, your constant Companion, your Counselor, the One who is with you and in you?

It is uppermost on God's heart for us to get to know His greatness, His power, His day-by-day operating and working in our lives, His ability to work miracles.

Paul was in prison, very shortly to die. He was an old man and I think he had a premonition that he wasn't long for this world. Even after living for and with God many years, Paul still exclaimed, "For my determined purpose is that I may know Him—that I may progressively become more deeply and intimately acquainted with Him, perceiving and recognizing and understanding [the wonders of His person] more strongly and more clearly. And that I may in that same way come to know the power outflowing from His resurrection [which it exerts over believers] and that I may so share His sufferings as to be continually transformed [in spirit into His likeness even] to His death" (Phil. 3:10, AMP).

The Greek word used here for "know" is *ginōskō*. There are two significant implications in this word. First, it frequently suggests progress in knowledge—there is the realization on the part of the "knower" that he still has things to learn on the subject. Second, *ginōskō* frequently implies an active relationship between the one who knows and the person known; in this respect, what is known is of value and importance to the one who knows, and hence the establishment of the relationship. Paul was saying that after all he had gone through as a Christian, after all his experiences in walking with Christ, after all he had come to know about Him, his greatest desire, even as a man near death, was to know Christ better and to deepen his relationship with Him. "But whatever was to my profit I now consider loss for the sake of Christ. What is more, I consider everything a loss compared to the surpassing greatness of knowing Jesus Christ my Lord, for whose sake I have lost all things. I consider them rubbish, that I may gain Christ" (Phil. 3:7-8).

This is what God has on His heart for us.

As we go through the hours of the day, how often do our thoughts intermingle with His? He wants to be our Companion, but how frequently do we converse with Him? When the real storms of life come, we are apt to get on our knees before Him, but we tend to leave Him out of all the little happenings in our lives. He longs to be involved in *everything.*

One of George Mueller's prayers was, "Lord Jesus, the thing that is uppermost on my heart is to get to know You more and more and more and more."

Perhaps one reason we don't pray is that we don't see its true *value.*

The disciples faced the tyranny of the urgent in first-century garb when in ministering to the needs of the saints, they had no time for the most important aspects of their work:

> So the Twelve gathered all the disciples together and said, "It would not be right for us to neglect the ministry of the Word of God in order to wait on tables. Brothers, choose seven men from among you who are known to be full of the Spirit and wisdom. We will turn this responsibility over to them and will give our attention to prayer and the ministry of the Word" (Acts 6:2-4).

Dr. Bob Munger, author and pastor, said of this passage, "Prayer was not a tool to be used in the ministry. Prayer was the basis on which the total ministry was established."

For many years Carole and I had the privilege of colaboring with Dee Moen, a Navigator girls' worker who for the last years of her life was an invalid and had little strength. As I was visiting her one week, she asked, "Jack, where do I fit now that

I'm an invalid?" I had no answer at the time, but the very next week as I was reading 1 Chronicles 16:4, God showed me an answer for Dee. This verse says of David, "He appointed some of the Levites to minister before the ark of the Lord, to make petition, to give thanks, and to praise the Lord, the God of Israel."

I was so excited about this passage that the very next day, I went down to Dee's apartment, walked in, and asked, "Dee, are you familiar with 1 Chronicles 16:4?"

"No, I don't think so," she replied.

"Let me read it to you," I said. After I read it to her, I continued, "I wonder if now that you are confined to bed most of the time, your part in God's ministry is to petition, thank, and praise the Lord?"

Dee took that passage as her commission from God for the next few years. She became a prayer warrior *magna cum laude* for the kingdom of Jesus Christ. Without fail each day, Dee petitioned, thanked, and praised the Lord for many hours. It was her ministry and service to God. My guess is that when the rewards are bestowed before the throne of God, we will discover this was her *major* ministry in spite of the many lives she had touched in other ways.

I don't run into many people like Dee. Yet prayer is the *foundation* on which any ministry is built.

Prayer's Priority

A.J. Gordon said it well: "You can do more than pray after you have prayed, but you cannot do more than pray until you have prayed." It has been said, "If we would do much *for* God, we must ask much *of* God."

We "keep" ourselves "in God's love" by continually developing new areas of prayer. Several such areas have challenged me in recent years.

One which comes back to me time and again is the

command to pray without ceasing (1 Thes. 5:17). Luke (18:1) put it another way: "Then Jesus told His disciples a parable to show them that they should always pray and not give up." The NASB and RSV say "lose heart." I feel there is a direct relationship between the two—one either prays or gives up, loses heart, and faints.

In his classic little book called *Purpose in Prayer,* E.M. Bounds says, " 'Men ought always to pray' (Luke 18:1, KJV). 'Always' does not mean that we are to neglect the ordinary duties of life; what it means is that the soul which has come into intimate contact with God in the silence of the prayer chamber is never out of conscious touch with the Father, but the heart is always going out to Him in loving communion, and that the moment the mind is released from the task upon which it is engaged, it returns as naturally to God as the bird does to its nest."

This practice of the heart in prayer takes years to develop, but it is a goal worth working toward with all our strength. Praying without ceasing means to develop such an intimate walk with God that when our minds are freed from routine tasks, they automatically go back to God. It means that our response to every situation is, "What would You have me say or do, Father?" It means continual fellowship; an awareness of Christ's presence at all times. It means being aware we are in a three-way conversation when talking with another person; and in a two-way conversation when we are alone.

A note from friend Jim White carried this reminder: "We should carefully study our priorities in the apportioning of our time each day. Many hours, while not actually wasted, may be spent on matters of only secondary importance. A fool has been defined as one who has lost the proportion of things. Some of us have developed the unfortunate habit of becoming so engrossed in the secondary that there is little time left for the primary. Especially is this the case where prayer is concerned, and our adversary does all in his power to aid and abet."

He suggests, "Check your daily and weekly schedules to see whether you are making adequate time for the essentially spiritual exercises of the soul. See whether the best is being relegated to a secondary place by that which is good. Weigh carefully, in the light of eternity, the respective values of the opportunities and responsibilities that are claiming your attention. Omit altogether, or give a very minor place to, the things of minor importance. Follow John Wesley's counsel: 'Never be unemployed, and never be triflingly employed.' And what higher employment can there be than communicating with the eternal God?"

Major Decisions

Another area God reminds me about often is developing the constant practice of praying regarding major decisions. Most decisions need to be prayed about of course, but major ones need to be bathed in prayer. Before the Lord Jesus faced one of the major decisions of His life—the selection of the Twelve— He spent *all night* praying about it (Luke 6:12).

When was the last time you spent all night, or even half a night, taking a major decision you had to make to God?

On August 6, 1976, Charles Blair, pastor of one of the largest churches in Denver, was tried and found guilty on 17 counts of fraudulent and otherwise prohibited sales of securities. Through a series of unfortunate decisions, this man who had walked with God found himself arrested, tried, fined, and placed on five years' probation. Why?

Charles Blair commented on his dream and vision for a Life Retirement Center to his wife one evening and of that incident said:

> But when that night, in the seclusion of our bedroom, I related the day's experiences, she [Betty, his wife] once again failed to catch the vision. She was sitting in her green overstuffed chair, the book she had been reading open in her lap.

"It seems to me, Charles, that you're already stretched to the breaking point. Where will you find time to listen to God when you're already working 26 hours a day?"

It was a bucket of cold water thrown on the fire of my excitement, and I came up sputtering. "How long do you have to listen, when the need's in front of your nose? Aren't we told to take care of the widows and orphans?"

How long do you have to listen. . . . So often, in the years ahead, I was to wish I had heeded my own question! *As long as necessary,* I should have answered, *to be absolutely certain it is His voice you hear.*

"No one argues with the need, dear," Betty was saying gently. "The question is whether it has our name on it. Do you remember, Charles, when you were so sure we were to go to Manila? And what Mr. Perkin said: 'It isn't the need we see around us; it's finding God's will for each life.' "*

In summarizing the lessons he learned in listening, Charles Blair relates: "I spent too much time reasoning, not enough in storming heaven. When time is short, the most important way we can use it is in prayer. In any crisis there comes a time when human logic is worthless. Then we need the tools which are available to us as children of God. More-than-usual *doing* must be balanced with more-than-usual *praying.*"

Another area often neglected is prayer related to the harvest. The Lord Jesus Himself commanded, "The harvest is plentiful but the workers are few. Ask the Lord of the harvest, therefore, to send out workers into His harvest field" (Matt 9:37-38). Once Christ himself prayed five times concerning "those whom You

---

*Charles Blair, with John and Elizabeth Sherrill, *The Man Who Could Do No Wrong,* © 1981 by Charles Blair. Published by Chosen Books, Lincoln, VA 22078, p. 218. Used by permission.

gave Me" (John 17:6)—those who were the laborers for the harvest.

If we are really serious in wanting to get involved with the harvest, we must first pray. As Paul told Timothy, "I urge, then, *first of all,* that requests, prayers, intercession, and thanksgiving be made for everyone" (1 Tim. 2:1, author's italics). Down through the ages, we are still being urged, "First of all," pray.

Prayer for Leading

Larry and Joan Blake went to Argentina in August, 1972 as representatives for The Navigators. After learning the language, they tried to talk with people about Christ but met with little success. After a year and a half in Argentina, Larry made the decision to work at the University of Buenos Aires, which seemed to offer the best opportunities. It was a school of 200,000 containing people who would be future leaders in the country.

However, the school, in a city with a greater metropolitan population of 9 million people, which takes two and a half hours to drive across, has no campus and is contained in 10 huge buildings located around the city. About 95 percent of the students live at home and take buses to school. Larry was told by other groups of Christians that it was probably impossible to work with students under those conditions. The situation looked dim.

But Larry felt that God was leading him to these students. One clear morning in the summer of 1975 Larry got out a map, went to all 10 of the buildings around the city, and walked around each one praying Joshua 1:3, "I will give you every place where you set your foot." He prayed, "God, give us people from this university."

After praying, Larry felt he should concentrate his efforts on the Engineering and Agronomy schools, primarily because the two buildings which housed those schools each had a space between the front door and the street. Most of the schools were in buildings located so close to the street and the buses that the students were gone before anyone could talk with them. But the engineering building had long steps leading down to the street, and the agronomy building had a parking lot between it and the street so there was space to stop and talk with people.

Larry claimed Isaiah 41:17: "The poor and needy search for water, but there is none; their tongues are parched with thirst. But I the Lord will answer them; I, the God of Israel, will not forsake them." Larry asked for two things: (a) that God would give him people who were seeking God and (b) that those people would live close to where Larry lived because a two-and-a-half hour drive for follow-up wasn't practical.

Larry and a friend began a survey of the students. As the students flooded out of the doors after class, Larry prayed to be guided to the ones God wanted him to speak to. If a student seemed interested, Larry would invite him to go across the street to a coffee bar and talk further. Then he would set up another appointment with that student or invite him to a study of the Gospel of John.

After two and a half months of interviews, Larry had 30 people in Bible study, which was all he and his friend could handle. Of those, all but one lived within 20 minutes of his home! These 30 became the initial bunch from which a strong band of Christians grew.

One verse he prayed frequently was Isaiah 41:20: "So that people may see and know, may consider and understand, that the hand of the Lord has done this, that the Holy One of Israel has created it." He wrote beside this verse in the margin of his Bible, "Lord, do what You do in and through me in such a way that You receive the glory." God did exactly that in a humanly "impossible" situation.

Prayer's Payoff

C. S. Todd, in his tract, "The Intercessory Missionary," tells of a discovery he made while looking through the records of the work carried on in the past by the China Inland Mission. He was struck by the fact that in one of these stations the number and spiritual character of the converts had far exceeded anyone's expectation. It could not be accounted for by the consecration of the missionaries who were employed at that particular place, for equally consecrated men had been in charge of similar but less fruitful areas of service. The rich harvest of souls remained a mystery, he said, until Hudson Taylor, on a visit to England, discovered the secret power which had resulted in such astonishing accomplishments. At the close of one of his messages, a gentleman from the audience came forward to meet him. In the conversation which followed, Hudson Taylor was surprised at the accurate knowledge the man possessed concerning this inland China station. "How is it," Mr. Taylor asked, "that you are so conversant with the conditions of that work?"

"Oh," he replied, "the missionary there and I are old college mates, and for four years we have regularly corresponded; he has sent me the names of inquirers and converts, and these I have daily taken to God in prayer." Suddenly Hudson Taylor saw the reason for the abundant harvest which had been gleaned at this one outpost for Christ: *The spiritual intercession of a truly dedicated man at home, praying definitely and daily for specific needs, had abounded to the glory of God.*

In a recent visit to our daughter and son-in-law in Guanajuato, Mexico, Tim asked us to pray especially on Tuesdays.

We asked, "Why Tuesdays?"

He explained that on Tuesday nights he met personally with a young Mexican who had been saved out of a life of demonism and the occult. "On Tuesdays Satan seems to try everything in the book to defeat my own life and the family—even illness and accidents to prevent me from getting together with this man for personal Bible study." You may be sure our "Tuesday praying" is fervent.

E. M. Bounds reflects, "Our prayer chamber should have our freshest strength, our calmest time, its hours unfettered, without obtrusion, without haste. Private place and plenty of time are the life of prayer."

How does your prayer life stack up with that statement? How does mine?

It all boils down to the fact that the aim of all real praying is to get things prayed for, as the child's cry for bread has for its end the getting of bread.

Prayer has been described as "the occupation of the heart with God." If we have a heart that truly is occupied with Him, it will be a heart which will be praying always, one that will not faint, and one that will have a vision of what God has on His heart.

6

Build Yourself in Faith—Your Focus

If you have to be stuck someplace, the Zurich Airport isn't bad—comfortable lounges, intriguing shops, and people of every language and race to observe.

Still, Carole and I wondered about the delay of our Swiss Air flight to Ghana—wondered, that is, until we took the time to read the newspapers we had been too busy to glance at during the previous two weeks of travel. Then it all fell into place.

We were to fly to Africa on a DC-10. But at that time, in 1979, all DC-10s had been grounded because of several crashes involving those aircraft. Every DC-10 was being carefully checked the world over.

Many people frantically switched to other carriers. Even though we knew and had confidence in the man responsible for sales of DC-10s and had flown on them a number of times before, we boarded with some anxiety. The nearly empty plane didn't alleviate our concerns. But we knew that the only way to build trust in that aircraft was to get on board. Each flight on a DC-10 in the following months built our confidence until today we rarely give it a thought.

If one never steps into airplanes, one will never learn to trust them.

How to Trust

Something of the same thing is true with God. The analogy isn't very good really, because on rare occasions planes do crash and so belie our trust. God on the other hand is completely trustworthy. Our steadfast hope in Him will never come to ruin. But in order to build our trust in His faithfulness, we have to step out in dependence on God much as we stepped into that DC-10.

Once again, the responsibility rests with us to take action. We are commanded, "Build yourselves up in your most holy faith" (Jude 20). In order to do that we must be dedicated to the task of learning to deliberately focus on Christ. We must endure no matter what happens, and finally we must depend on experiencing God's enabling grace.

Recently I read this little story:

The wheels of the heavily loaded Cessna 206 had barely left the wet jungle airstrip. The pilot had the throttle pushed all the way to the firewall. He had done this many times before and was confident they would clear the huge trees.

Then, as nearly as we can tell, the passenger sitting next to him had a surge of panic. He saw the onrushing trees filling the windshield. Fearful they were going to crash, he tried to help.

His intentions were good. "What's wrong with the pilot? Why doesn't he pull back on the controls?" The passenger apparently took hold of the flight controls and pulled back.

But it doesn't work that way. You have to build up airspeed before you point the nose skyward. Otherwise you stall.

The airplane pitched up, lost critical airspeed, and began to settle toward the jungle. The pilot wrenched the controls back and tried desperately to get the nose down. But it was too late. As the plane reached stalling speed the heavy engine pulled the nose over sharply and it spun to earth.

By God's grace, no one was killed, but all were injured, the pilot most seriously. Another plane happened to be on the ground, and its pilot rescued the injured. All were taken to a small jungle hospital where they eventually recovered.

There seem to be a lot of crashes these days because people can't keep their hands off the controls. I sympathize with the passenger, for I have a way of doing exactly the same thing in my spiritual journey. Thinking I know best, I try to take over and run things my way. It never works. Even Jesus had to submit to God's flight plan. "Not My will, but Thine be done" (Luke 22:42, KJV).

Things may seem mighty awkward—or scary—but we have to be willing to leave the controls in the hands of the Pilot.

It's the only way to fly.*

Every one of us is going to be guilty of trying to wrench the controls from our Pilot unless we have implicit faith in both His ability and His concern. In all of life we need a built-in confidence of our Saviour's *faithful*ness and His *able*ness.

In the first part of Hebrews 12 we read:

Therefore, since we are surrounded by such a great cloud of witnesses, let us throw off everything that hinders and the sin that so easily entangles, and let us run with perseverance the race marked out for us. Let us fix our eyes on Jesus, the Author

---

*By Bernie May, from *Beyond,* Feb./Mar. 1976, Jungle Aviation and Radio Service, Inc., Box 248, Waxhow, NC 28173.

and Perfecter of our faith, who for the joy set before Him endured the cross, scorning its shame, and sat down at the right hand of the throne of God. Consider Him who endured such opposition from sinful men, so that you will not grow weary and lose heart (vv. 1-3).

Whenever a "therefore" is found in Scripture, one needs to look what it is *there for*. In this case the "therefore" refers to the witnesses of the previous chapter.

God's Hall of Fame

Step into the vast room on whose walls are hung pictures of the great people in God's Hall of Fame. Some faces and names are readily recognized. See, there are Noah, Abraham, and Sarah. And look over there—Moses and Joseph. Yet many, hung just as prominently, are people we do not recognize. Under their pictures we read the reasons why they are displayed alongside the great patriarchs of the faith in this honored place:

Who shut the mouths of lions, quenched the fury of the flames, and escaped the edge of the sword; whose weakness was turned to strength; and who became powerful in battle and routed foreign armies. Women received back their dead, raised to life again. Others were tortured and refused to be released, so that they might gain a better resurrection. Some faced jeers and flogging, while still others were chained and put in prison. They were stoned; they were sawed in two; they were put to death by the sword. They went about in sheepskins and goatskins, destitute, persecuted, and mistreated—the world was not worthy of them (Heb. 11:33-38).

These stand as a great host of people who have gone on before us and testified to the fact that God is faithful—that He is in control of every situation and that He will never leave us.

They lived by this truth and dared stare death in the face regardless of the circumstances in which they found themselves.

The writer adds, "And what more shall I say? I do not have time to tell about Gideon, Barak, Samson, Jephthah, David, Samuel, and the prophets" (11:32).

The writer seems to have run out of breath. Can you imagine not having time to tell of David? Of Samson? I am sure they are among those in that great hall, but there just was no time to tell about them!

In one paragraph we read of women who received back their dead, raised to life again by faith (v. 35). That's the part we like to remember.

But the next sentence tells of God's people who by faith were tortured and refused to be released. That's the part we would like to forget. Many did *not* receive "what had been promised" (v. 39) but hung on through suffering beyond our ability to comprehend until they died. It was only after death that they saw the fulfillment of God's promise.

Joni Eareckson often tells how, in the first years after she became a quadriplegic, she prayed to be among the first group of people described in Hebrews 11—the ones who were healed, raised, and became powerful.

It was her friend Steve who reminded her that the Greek word for the power of God—*dunamis*—is the root word for both dynamite, explosive energy, and dynamo—controlled, useful engery. He said, "A healing experience would be like an explosive release of God's energy getting you out of the chair. But staying in the chair takes power too—controlled energy flowing through you that makes it possible to cope."*

---

*Joni, by Joni Eareckson, World Wide Publications, Minneapolis, MN 55403, p. 160.

Five Kinds of Healing

There are at least five different kinds of healing in the Bible:
(1) There is instantaneous healing such as we find when Christ
raised Lazarus from the dead (John 11). (2) Progressive healing
is another method Christ used to perform a miracle with one
blind man (Mark 8:22-26). (3) There is healing done through
someone else, as God healed Saul from his blindness through
Ananias (Acts 9). (4) Yet another way is the healing grace
which is given when God decides *not* to heal a physical disabili-
ty. This is found in 2 Corinthians 12:9 where three times Paul
asked God to take away his thorn in the flesh, but God replied,
"My grace is sufficient for you, for My power is made perfect
in weakness." The thorn was not removed, but God gave healing grace to give Paul victory in the midst of his pain. (5) The
last kind of healing is the healing of all our pains and disabilities
in the final immortal, glorified body we will receive one day.

Joni now believes that she is only going to experience healing in heaven, as was true of the people mentioned in the later
part of Hebrews 11.

What was the secret of these people's steadfast faith?

Their focus was on the living, triune God—the God who
never promised a trouble-free life, but who promised instead to
go through their troubles with them.

The story is told of a small boy who had to have corrective
surgery on both legs and for months had to continually wear
braces on both legs night and day in order that his bones would
be re-formed properly. Many nights he would cry pitifully because of his pain. "Mommy, Mommy," he would weep. "I can't
stand it anymore. Please take the braces off for a while. Please,
Mommy, please. I just can't take it any longer."

"I can't take the braces off, Honey," his mother would reply.

"Oh, Mommy, please. It hurts so bad. Take them off please,"
he would beg pathetically.

With tears in her eyes, his mother would say, "Son, I can't

take them off. But I will lie in bed with you and hold you in my arms and cry with you."

God is like that! He knows in His sovereignty that to "take the braces off"—to keep us from pain and trouble—would leave us disfigured, maimed. But He will stay by our side, hold us in His arms, and weep with us. If we focus on Him—"considering Him who endured" (Heb. 12:3)—no trial will be too difficult to bear.

Run Light

But in order to focus on Jesus, we must get rid of our distractions. We are to "throw off everything that hinders" (12:1).

Paul uses the analogy of a runner in the Olympic games and his need to take off every possible bit of weight which could hinder his winning.

One guideline for running in a race is to run light. If you are just out jogging, your sweat suit and heavy shoes aren't important. But if you want to win—to complete a race triumphantly—then you lay aside everything that would hinder and any trailing garment you might trip on. Scripture even tells you what some of those weighed-down concerns are. "Be careful, or your hearts will be weighed down with dissipation, drunkenness, and the anxieties of life," Jesus said (Luke 21:34). A weight is *anything* that hinders us from going anywhere, doing any job God might ask of us.

Suppose God asked you to take a job in Brazil next month. What might come to your mind as reasons you couldn't go that soon, if at all? For many the word that flashes to mind is "debt"—a terrible weight in running our spiritual race.

Recently we heard of a young man who really wanted to be "mobile" for Christ. Yet he was seriously considering marrying a woman whose heart was in this world. She wanted him to get a second job in order to save for a home. In this case, if he decides to marry her, his wife, the second job, and the home will become "weights."

Now please don't misunderstand me. A wife and home aren't necessarily weights! (I hope not—I've got both!) But *anything* that doesn't have God's stamp of approval on it for our lives may be a weight—sometimes things that are good in themselves are wrong at a given moment.

Activities to which we say "yes" hastily, ministries which do not have our names on them, problems not turned over to God—all can be weights. So can doubt, pride, slothful living. To "lay aside the weight" means to put away that which would hinder our relationship with God or stop us from becoming the kind of persons God wants us to be, or doing what He wants us to do.

A little booklet that is a constant challenge to me is Charles Hummel's *The Tyranny of the Urgent.* He says, "Several years ago an experienced cotton-mill manager said to me, 'Your greatest danger is letting the urgent things crowd out the important.' He didn't realize how hard his maxim hit. . . . We live in constant tension between the urgent and the important. The problem is that the important task rarely must be done today, or even this week. Extra hours of prayer and Bible study, a visit with that non-Christian friend, careful study of an important book; these projects can wait. But the urgent tasks call for instant action—endless demands pressure us every hour and every day.

"A man's home is no longer his castle; it is no longer a place away from urgent tasks because the telephone breaches the walls with imperious demands. The momentary appeal of these tasks seems irresistible and important, and they devour our energy. But in the light of time's perspective their deceptive prominence fades; with a sense of loss we recall the important tasks pushed aside. We realize we've become slaves to the tyranny of the urgent."

A weight—or multiple weights—can be heavy upon us when we yield to the pressures of the urgent without grave consideration to what is truly important in our lives.

The other thing I need to lay aside is "the sin that so easily entangles." Another translation speaks of "the easily besetting sin." And still another, "the easily encompassing (or surrounding) sin." The concept here reminds one of a ring of wild beasts in the jungle that encircle a campfire at night, each ready to pounce on a careless victim.

Periodically each of us needs a time of self-examination in the light of Psalm 132:23-24: "Search me, O God, and know my heart; test me and know my anxious thoughts. See if there is any offensive way in me, and lead me in the way everlasting." The King James Version says "wicked way" but perhaps "offensive" brings areas to the surface that we haven't thought about as clinging sins. How often our lives are hindered—our ministries rendered ineffective—by traits of stubbornness (we call it stick-to-itiveness or conviction), callousness (we call it objectivity), a sharp tongue (we call it honesty), an untamed imagination (we all it creativity). "So watch out that the sunshine isn't blotted out. If you are filled with light within, *with no dark corners,* then your face will be radiant too, as though a floodlight is beamed upon you" (Luke 11:35-36, TLB, author's italics).

Christ's Home

Dr. Bob Munger in his classic message, *My Heart—Christ's Home* talks about the different rooms in the house of his life and how Christians need to allow Christ to take possession of their entire homes. After each room has been turned over to the Lord, he finds there is something else he needs to deal with. He says:

There is just one more matter that I might share with you. One day I found Him [Christ] waiting for me at the door. There was an arresting look in His eye. He said to me as I entered, "There is a peculiar odor in the house. There is something dead around here. It's upstairs. I think it is in the hall closet." As soon as He said the words, I knew what He was talking about. Yes, there was a small hall closet up there on the landing, just a few feet square, and in that closet behind lock and key, I had one or two little personal things that I did not want anybody to know about and certainly I did not want Christ to see. I knew they were dead and rotting things. And yet I loved them, and I wanted them so for myself that I was afraid to admit they were there. I went up the stairs with Him and as we mounted, the odor became stronger and stronger. He pointed at the door and said, "It's in there! Some dead thing!"

I was angry. That's the only way I can put it. I had given Him access to the library, the dining room, the drawing room, the workshop, the rumpus room, and now He was asking me about a little two-by-four closet. I said inwardly, "This is too much. I am not going to give Him the key."

"Well," He said, reading my thoughts, "if you think I am going to stay up here on the second floor with this odor, you are mistaken. I will take My bed out on the back porch. I'm certainly not going to put up with that." And I saw Him start down the stairs.

When you have come to know and love Christ, the worst thing that can happen is to sense His fellowship retreating from you. I had to surrender. "I'll give You the key," I said sadly, "but You'll have to open the closet. You'll have to clean it out. I haven't the strength to do it."

"I know," He said. "I know you haven't. Just give Me the key. Just authorize Me to take care of that closet and I will." So, with trembling fingers I passed the key over to Him. He took it from my hand, walked over to the door, opened it, and entered it, took out all the putrefying stuff that was rotting there, and threw it away. Then He cleansed the closet, painted it, fixed it up, doing it all in a moment's time. Oh, what victory and release to have that dead thing out of my life!*

We need to turn our "closets"—our "dark corners"—over to Christ so that He can cleanse them and make them pure. Then our lives will be radiant.

Besides adding weights and sins, we tend to lose sight of the goal. Our focus fades, our attention wavers, and our footsteps falter. It may be that the race itself becomes so exciting that we lose sight of the finish. Or a giant obstacle confronts us and we swerve to avoid it, getting sidetracked in the process. Or we may be knocked down by an unexpected blow and feel like quitting the race. Or we just get *tired.* We don't endure because we haven't kept sight of the goal.

Our focus—our attention—must be on Jesus. As our focal point, the center of our lives, He will then encourage us and be our example.

But *how* do we focus on Jesus? The "how" goes arrow-like back to the basics of our Christian life—our time in the Word and in prayer and our immediate obedience when He speaks.

One of the results of setting our eyes on Jesus through the Scriptures and prayer is that more and more we will recognize who He really is—our sovereign Lord. "Sovereignty" is a big word with a bigger meaning. Yet so much of life and actions hinge on it. Sovereign means above or superior to all others, chief, greatest, supreme. Supreme in power, rank, and authority.

"Supreme in power." Our minds need to be gripped with the magnitude of that truth. Practically, sovereignty means that nothing is too big for God to handle; nothing is too small for Him to bother with. It means He is in total control of every

---

*Taken from *My Heart—Christ's Home,* by Robert Boyd Munger. © 1954 by Inter-Varsity Christian Fellowship of the USA and used by permission of InterVarsity Press, Downers Grove, IL 60515.

event of our lives. Do we believe it? I mean, do we *really* believe it?

If so, we can face life with our heads held high, our eyes straight ahead, focusing on the Master of our lives, Jesus Christ.

7

Build Yourself in Faith—Your Attitudes and Actions

Recently our minister opened his message with the following story. Several weeks earlier I'd read it in the cartoon section of the Sunday paper. This kind of story is not easily pushed from one's mind.

A man was walking along a narrow path, not paying much attention to where he was going when suddenly, he slipped and fell over the edge of a cliff. As he fell, he grabbed a branch growing from the side of the cliff. Realizing that he couldn't hang on for long, he called desperately for help.

MAN: Is anybody up there?

VOICE: Yes, I'm here.

MAN: Who are you?

VOICE: The Lord.

MAN: Lord, help me!

VOICE: Do you trust Me?

MAN: I trust you completely, Lord.

VOICE: Good. Let go of the branch.

MAN: What????

VOICE: I said, "Let go of the branch."

MAN (after a long pause): Is anybody *else* up there?

Faith is a sure belief that has to be acted upon. If we are not willing to act upon it, we don't have it.

To develop faith, we must have the attitude of a learner—a disciple. If we are "trained by discipline"—and we are (Heb. 12:7-11)—then we have to be open to God's training, alert to His lessons, learning and absorbing constantly.

But blocks to a learning attitude are multiple. Three of the great enemies of a Christian that can put him on the shelf are pride, money, and lust.

Pride

The subtleness of pride, even in a ministry that God is blessing, can take over a believer's heart until he no longer thinks, "I can do everything through Him [Christ] who gives me strength" (Phil. 4:13). Instead he thinks, "*I* can do it. With my talent and ability and a little bit of help from God along the way, I can do it."

In one of Charles Blair's "lessons on listening" he warns, "Beware of prior successes. The success of yesterday tempts us to lean on a formula rather than on God. Moses struck the rock with his staff and water gushed forth. When he tried to provide water the same way a second time, God reproved him. Faith is progressive. At Calvary Temple we mixed fund-raising with borrowing, successfully. At Life Center we repeated this mix—to our sorrow. We weren't allowing God to take us another step in discipleship."*

Pride is not always shown by an exalted sense of our self-worth, of course. Sometimes pride is seen in excessive shyness, the I-can't-do-anything syndrome. An extreme introvert may be proud, if he is obsessed with self, which is an inverted form of pride.

---

*Charles Blair, *The Man Who Could Do No Wrong,* page 232.

Money

Money can block our goal from sight. Our faith in God's faithfulness is imperative. If we are not careful, we can get too "comfortable." We can become too concerned with the cares of this world. We may even preach sermons on holding possessions rather than letting possessions hold us. We may wax eloquent about gripping things lightly rather than tightly—so all God has to do is touch our hands for us to release them. But as we get older and experience His blessing and His prosperity, it may become easier to trust in our investments than in God.

Lust

And then there is lust. It starts with a thought—just one—that isn't immediately brought into captivity (2 Cor. 10:5). When we fail to bring that thought under the Holy Spirit's control, there comes a second thought. We begin to dabble and play around with sin vicariously in our minds. And too often, as was David's experience, the thought becomes a look, graduates into an act, and results in a ruined life. When desire and opportunity meet, they often result in sin.

Learners and Endurers

People can be learners at 101. Or can stop learning at 20. I am talking about learning lessons from God through various means He has at His disposal, not the mere acquisition of knowledge. God uses His Word, people, and life itself to nail His lessons onto the blocks of our lives. Are we determined to be learners?

Our attitudes must be that of learners, our actions those of endurance—with our eyes on Jesus—with the end in view of knowing Christ better and becoming conformed to His image.

Dr. V. Raymond Edman, who was the president of Wheaton College when I attended there, spoke every year on the subject, "It's always too soon to quit." He usually presented this message as midterm examinations were in progress and a wave of discouragement was rippling over the freshman class. This-is-so-tough-it-can't-be-worth-it type of thoughts washed over minds, leaving the dirty debris of despair. Dr. Edman's message was timely and true. At times the Christian life *is* a matter of simply refusing to quit.

We read of the early missionaries to India and parts of Africa who packed their belongings in their coffins as they went to preach the Gospel of Christ in a pioneering ministry. They had no furloughs, no hospitals or medical knowledge or medicines to prevent what they knew to be almost inevitable: sickness, disease, and death. But they went forth—and endured.

If we really believe that God is on the throne of our lives, that He is walking on the waters of every situation, that He has not taken a vacation, gone to sleep, or taken a break from controlling each moment, then we will endure. We will refuse to quit.

Grace and Mercy

But the ability to focus our attention on Christ, our action to endure and to maintain a learner's attitude, are only possible in the light of God's *grace.*

Many times we think of grace only in connection with salvation—"by grace you have been saved" (Eph. 2:8-9). But that aspect of God's grace is only the *beginning.* The "riches of His grace" are beyond our comprehension (Eph. 1:5-8; 2:7). And we are commanded to "be strong in the grace that is in Christ Jesus" (2 Tim. 2:1).

Have you thought lately about the "riches of His grace"? According to Paul (Eph. 3:8) these riches are unfathomable. If God says we can't fathom them, our list will never be complete. But what are *some?*

I heard the testimony of a sharp young executive some time ago. He said that several years ago he found himself hundreds of thousands of dollars in debt, his marriage falling apart, and his world coming unglued at the seams. Driving home one night, he got behind a rickity old station wagon which looked like it would shake into a pile of junk any minute. But on the back was a bumper sticker (he had a *thing* against bumper stickers) which arrested his attention and which he couldn't get out of his mind. It read: GOD IS IN CONTROL.

That was the beginning of his search—and his finding—God.

The knowledge of that truth in a world sick and angry and hurting is one of God's greatest riches to me!

We can list many others. But my question is this: Does the wonderful truth of God's unfathomable riches *grip your soul?* Or are you reading this with a "ho-hum-I-know—isn't-it-nice" feeling? Let's ask God for an insurgence of overwhelming gratitude—a feeling of awe and wonder at His greatness, His goodness, His riches that He has lavished on us! If thankfulness is not controlling our hearts, it is little wonder we lose patience at a flat tire, a long grocery line, or a blister on our foot.

Grace is ours to have in abundance. But just how do we appropriate what God has freely given us?

Prayer is one way. "Let us then approach the throne of grace with confidence, so that we may receive mercy and find *grace* to help us in our time of need" (Heb. 4:16).

First, we obtain mercy—which means being spared from receiving what we deserve, God's wrath and condemnation. No penalty is exacted because Christ paid for all our sins. "Because of the Lord's great love [or mercy] we are not consumed, for His compassions never fail" Jeremiah tells us (Lam. 3:22).

After God's mercy, we often obtain grace—receiving that which we do *not* deserve, His riches. We find "grace to help us in our time of need."

Grace is given in proportion to and at the time of our needs. The bigger a need, the more grace we experience. We *need* to obtain God's mercy or we would die in our sins. We *have* to find His grace or we live in spiritual poverty.

Often in life, forgiveness—mercy—comes first and *then* you

need and can expect His grace. Because of your sinful nature or perhaps your own stupidity, you may do foolish things that displease the Lord. You find yourself in a hole of your own making and you cry out to God for His mercy, His forgiveness. Then you claim 1 John 1:9: "If we confess our sins, He is faithful and just and will forgive us our sins and purify us from all unrighteousness."

Now you are forgiven, but you are still in the same hole. Then you say, "Lord, I can never get through this by myself. I need Your help, Your strengthening hand. Help me and give me some ideas of what I can do to please You."

When Carole and I had been married about five years we moved into the first house we'd ever lived in. Our first four years had been in seminary where we lived in a 27-foot trailer with a path to the bath! Then we progressed to a one-bedroom apartment with all borrowed furniture. After that we found ourselves in a rented three-bedroom house in Portland without any furniture. We were so excited about it that, without really giving much thought or prayer to it, we bought some bedroom and living room furniture and a carpet. We didn't have any money but the bank and the Mayhalls now owned this furniture.

At the end of the first week as we sat there looking at our new possessions, both of us began feeling strange inside. We had never been in debt before—it was a new experience for us. The more we thought about it, the more miserable we felt. As we started praying about it, we realized we had been presumptuous. We had done this without consulting the Lord. Four hundred dollars worth. (You better believe furniture was a lot cheaper in those days—but $400 was a lot bigger too!) Day after miserable day that $400 cloud hung over our heads and we didn't know what to do with it.

Finally, we got down on our knees and admitted our sin to God, asking Him to forgive us. Ours was a sin of presumptuousness and was done out of ignorance rather than disobedience—but it was *sin.*

Then we asked, "Lord, what do we do now to get this right with the world and with You?" Even though we'd confessed our sin, we still owed $400 and the furniture store wouldn't take back the things we had used. The payments were more than we could afford on our salary.

We began to ask the Lord for ideas. Our first brilliant one was to ask the Lord to dump the $400 into our laps to pay off the bank. But God knew we wouldn't learn the lessons we needed to learn if He did it that way. We prayed about this for several days.

At this point, we had obtained *mercy*—we knew God had forgiven us. What we needed now was *grace* to get out of this bind.

Simultaneously, Carole and I came across a passage that spoke to us: "Therefore I tell you, do not worry about your life, what you will eat or drink; or about your body, what you will wear. Is not life more important than food, and the body more important than clothes? Look at the birds of the air; they do not sow or reap or store away in barns, and yet your heavenly Father feeds them. Are you not much more valuable than they?" (Matt. 6:25-26) This passage concludes, "But seek first His kingdom and His righteousness, and all these things will be given to you as well" (v. 33).

Our problem right then was being anxious and worrying. Carole and I both saw this passage was God's promise to take care of our food and clothing. In this passage He promised to meet the needs of His children in those two areas.

We had enough clothing for a few months but food was another matter. Nevertheless, God led us to take the paycheck I got once a month and pay all the other bills first. Then whatever was left would be put toward the $400 debt. We were going to trust Him for food and clothing.

I am not recommending this procedure to anyone else without God's specific guidance, but God made His way very clear in this instance to us.

I cannot begin to tell you all that happened. No one else knew of our decision or our need. But amazing things transpired. We found a sack of groceries on our back porch; received a Valentine with a check from a person we had never heard from before—or since. One day I was downtown and found a wallet which had $60 in it! It also had the owner's name in it. I got on the phone and called the man to tell him I'd found his wallet. He said, "Oh, Man, that's terrific. Was there any money in it?"

I said, "Yes, $60."

Long silence. "Is that right? I'll be right over and get it."

He came over and insisted we take a $10 reward. (We didn't argue too hard!)

Right in the middle of this time I had an emergency appendectomy—and we had no insurance. The day I left the hospital two men from the church, without knowing our need, put into my hands gifts which exactly covered it. The same day the doctor's bill arrived, we received a rebate on our income tax which matched it.

This type of thing happened week after week after week for the six months it took to pay off that $400—and then it stopped completely. We didn't need it anymore.

The grace of God can meet your every need. Perhaps your need is for a joyous spirit, victory over a sin, wisdom in a decision to really know the will of God, or a need for encouragement because of failure. His grace will provide anything. Everything. His promise is: " 'My grace is sufficient for you, for My power is made perfect in weakness.' Therefore I will boast all the more gladly about my weaknesses, so that Christ's power may rest on me" (2 Cor. 12:9). What a promise!

His grace is great enough to meet the great things—
 The crashing waves that overwhelm the soul,
The roaring winds that leave us stunned and breathless,
 The sudden storms beyond our life's control.

His grace is great enough to meet the small things—
 The little pin-prick troubles that annoy,
The insect worries, buzzing and persistent,
 The squeaking wheels that grate upon our joy.
                              —Annie Johnson Flint

To build ourselves in the most holy faith (Jude 20), we must keep the focus of our attention on Christ, have the attitude of learners, take the action of endurance, and experience the grace of God. It's the only way to fly!

8

Build Yourself
by Knowing God's Will

I sat in the park, a great cloud of gloom hovering directly overhead, dimming the bright August afternoon. If Dilemma had been the name of the game, Confusion was the umpire and I was being scored against in every inning.

"What *should* I do? Lord, *what* should I do? What should I *do?*" I was crying internally. But the scoreboard showed ZERO in my answer column.

I had been deliberating on my situation for several hours without result as I reviewed the circumstances which led me here.

I had taken a job as youth director at a church in a midwestern city right after graduating from seminary. But after being there a little over a year, it had become clear in June that I should resign as of September 1. I wasn't too concerned about another job as we began to pray about God's next step for us. It was clear through a set of circumstances and God's leading in our hearts that He was directing us out of this job, so I knew He had something else for us. We started investigating ministry opportunities, but June and July came and went, and nothing opened up.

One day Carole and I ran into some old friends we hadn't seen since college days. He was the youth director of a church where we had attended a banquet. He and his wife were leaving September 1 to go to Africa as missionaries. The more we talked about a replacement for his job, the more interested I became. The church was growing in an exciting way, there was a tremendous young people's program already going on, and the pastor was a godly man. A new Christian education building was in the process of being built two blocks from a huge high school. Throw in a salary one and a half times what I was presently making, mix it all together, and one fantastic opportunity emerged!

We met with the pastor, the Christian education committee, and finally with the Board, and then received an invitation to minister with that church beginning September 1. Perfect.

God's Will

But as we began to pray about the job in earnest, there was a strange "blah" in my spirit. And nothing—blank—from the Lord. I read the Bible but received no leading. Finally the pastor called and said, "Jack, we believe you are God's man for the job—that this is God's will for you and we need to have an answer this week."

I said "OK. I'll call you in two days and let you know."

Which forced me to the park that sunny August afternoon.

Now how do you discern the will of God in a situation like this? It is one of the "gray areas" of life and I detest gray areas!

Positive commands abound in Scripture—the "Thou shalts" of the Bible. Often we have trouble *obeying* them, but we don't have any difficulty knowing what they are. They are clear and plain to comprehend.

For instance, we never have to ask if it is God's will to be *thankful* in spirit. The Word says, "Give thanks in all circumstances, for this is God's will for you in Christ Jesus" (1 Thes.

5:18). Thanking God for the difficulties as well as the joys, for the tough decisions as well as the easy ones, is essential in order to be in the continuing will of God.

We are also to *listen* to God's voice daily. As the proverbist tells us: "Blessed is the man who listens to Me, watching daily at My doors, waiting at My doorway" (Prov. 8:34).

We are to *praise* God daily, call on Him daily, examine the Scriptures daily, and encourage one another daily*—and this is just a partial list of the many things the Lord wants us to do *every day*.

If I am consistently in the Scriptures, consistent in responding obediently to those areas about which He speaks to me, if I am to the best of my ability through the power of Christ attempting to put these things into practice each day, then *today* I am in the will of God. And tomorrow. And the next day. The next month. And next year. The same will be true 10 years from now. I will still be in the will of God if I obey Him *daily*.

Renewal

As Paul says: "I appeal to you therefore, brethren, by the mercies of God, to present your bodies as a living sacrifice, holy and acceptable to God, which is your spiritual worship. Do not be conformed to this world, but be transformed by the renewal of your mind, that you may prove what is the will of God, what is good and acceptable and perfect" (Rom. 12:1-2, RSV).

We are changed, or transformed, by our minds being renewed. This "renewal" doesn't happen at one given point in time, but is a process of exposing our minds to God through His Word. We are warned against being "conformed to this world" which also is a process that takes time. The renewal of

---

*Psalms 61:8; 88:9b; Acts 17:11 (the Berean church was commended for this); Hebrews 3:13.

one's mind takes place in direct proportion to the exposure of his heart to God's Word. As we go deep into His Word, we begin to think on God's wavelength. Our minds become more and more attuned to His way of thinking so that as much as possible, we are thinking on a parallel track with Him. Unless we completely steel ourselves against it, we become conformed to that which we are exposed to continually.

Carole and I have been married over 33 years and in many areas we know each other very well. I don't have to ask her if she likes a dessert that has coconut in it (she doesn't), how she likes her coffee (black), or if a certain song will bring tears to her eyes (it will). Over a period of time I have grown to know without asking her what she likes and dislikes. This knowing results in adjustments or "conforming."

The more our lives are saturated with God's Word and the more we begin to think as God thinks, our minds become renewed within. The end product is that we will prove or demonstrate or exemplify what is the will of God.

As we live with God, and expose ourselves to His thinking through His Word, we won't even have to ask Him for direction in many areas. We will just *know* what He wants.

But because the road of life consists of continuous forks, crossroads, and junctions for which there is no map, we have to listen to the Guide who knows our individual journeys. He wants to tell us which way to go at every point.

A person without Christ has nothing which compares with that! The best he can do is use his wits. He can look at a decision he is facing, take out a piece of paper and pen, draw a line down the middle and write PRO and CON at the top. He can write down all the things he can think of in favor of the decision in the PRO column and all the things against it on the CON side, draw a line across the bottom, add them up, and if the PROs outweigh the CONs, it's a good deal.

It isn't that the pros and cons should *not* be considered, but

I'm glad I don't have to run my life that way. No Christian has to. God has provided a much better way. Oh, it's a little scary. It involves faith. It entails the unknown, walking by faith and not by sight. But it is exciting. And it is sure.

God's Peace

Because I could find no Scripture to help in that decision about the job as a youth director at the park that day, I had to rely on one of the principles my Guide often uses in my life.

As I sat there on the park bench, I recalled that "God is not the author of confusion but of peace" (1 Cor. 14:33, KJV). In my heart was a confusion I knew was not of the Lord.

"Let the peace of Christ *rule* in your hearts, since as members of one body you were called to peace. And be thankful" (Col. 3:15) came to my mind. The word "rule" in the Greek means to be the umpire or referee of. You know what an umpire does. He calls a baseball pitch a "ball" or a "strike." He says a player is "out" or "safe." A good umpire is clear and decisive about his calls and decisions. There isn't a major league umpire who would last a day if some guy slid into third base and the umpire stood there pulling on his chin, saying, "Well, let's see, was he out or safe? I'll need to think about this for a while." God doesn't make that kind of fuzzy call either.

Doubts

I was reminded of the 14th chapter of Romans which deals with a gray issue. The Romans had written to ask Paul about whether they should eat meat which had been offered to idols (see also 1 Cor. 8). Paul didn't say yes or no, but dealt with the issue by stating a principle: If you have a lack of peace, an uneasiness, a lack of freedom, you should not do it. He summarized it in Romans 14:23: "But the man who has doubts is condemned if he eats, because his eating is not from faith; and everything that does not come from faith is sin."

DOUBT, written in capital letters, was the way I felt that afternoon in the park.

Oswald Chambers put it this way, "There are times when you cannot understand why you cannot do what you want to do. When God brings the blank space, see that you do not fill it in, but wait. . . . Never run before God's guidance. If there is the slightest doubt, then He is not guiding. Whenever there is doubt—*don't*."*

I came home, told Carole about my decision, and the next morning called the pastor. I said, "Look, this is a fantastic opportunity. I would love to work with you, but I have absolutely no peace in my heart to say yes. So I have to say no."

Did everything work out beautifully from that point? I wish I could say yes! But it didn't. September 1 came and went and I was jobless. I had a file folder full of correspondence from churches but nothing worked out.

For two months we lived with Carole's folks. To support us, I did everything from taking a "fruit tree" census for the government to leading singing for a week of revival services. Two months later we moved to California to sponge off my folks for a while. Dad was moving into a new store and I painted it for him. I remember vividly that the store had been a ghastly shade of red and needed four coats of new paint to cover it. Not exactly the type of job I had spent four years in seminary preparing for!

Every day we sought what God would have for us next. Yes, we got discouraged. We questioned if we had made a mistake—if I had been wrong about God's leading. After several weeks with no job, no income, and a wife and daughter to take care of, I wondered if we really had missed it! But God taught us a valuable lesson during this experience—to "never doubt in the dark what God has shown you in the light" (Dr. Edman

---

*My Utmost for His Highest, January 4.

also used to preach this message every year at Wheaton College). As I had prayed that afternoon in the park, the leading of God was crystal clear to me. God was saying no to the job. We just needed to hang on. God had led us and we had to trust Him.

Finally a letter came from a friend in Oregon telling us of a church needing a youth director, which eventually led us to Portland, working with Dr. Jack Mitchell. Dr. Jack had so impressed me when I had listened to him teach the special Bible lectures at seminary, that I had prayed we might have the privilege of working with him someday. I had almost forgotten about praying this when, after four months of waiting, God not only opened up His choice opportunity, but one that was an answer to a dream and prayer years before.

It was in Portland that we later ran into The Navigators, which God had chosen to be our life's work.

As I look back to that afternoon in the park praying for direction, I had no idea how important a decision that was. What if I had said yes despite my inner turmoil?

The peace of God will lead us in such a sure way that we cannot mistake it.

You might say, "But Jack, the peace of God is so nebulous for me. I need something more concrete than that. I want to be sure what God is planning for me and be positive I'm tuned in to His mind."

I can understand that.

Finding the peace of God takes some *time*.

Throw Out the Fleece?

So why don't we just "throw out the fleece" as Gideon did and get God's answer immediately? It's so much simpler! Or is it?

Let's take a look at the story of this "mighty man of valor," Gideon, as found in Judges 6.

> Then the angel of the Lord came and sat under the oak in Ophrah, that belonged to Joash the Abiezrite, where his son Gideon was threshing wheat in a winepress to keep it from the Midianites. When the angel of the Lord appeared to Gideon, he said, "The Lord is with you, mighty warrior."
>
> "But sir," Gideon replied, "if the Lord is with us, why has all this happened to us? Where are all His wonders that our fathers told us about when they said, 'Did not the Lord bring us up out of Egypt?' But now the Lord has abandoned us and put us into the hand of Midian."
>
> The Lord turned to him and said, "Go in the strength you have and save Israel out of Midian's hand. Am I not sending you?"
>
> "But Lord," Gideon asked, "how can I save Israel? My clan is the weakest in Manasseh, and I am the least in my family."
>
> The Lord answered, "I will be with you, and you will strike down the Midianites as if they were but one man."
>
> Gideon replied, "If now I have found favor in Your eyes, give me a sign that it is really You talking to me" (Jud. 6:11-17).

The Midianites had overrun the land and Israel was in bondage to them. When the Israelites raised a good crop of wheat, the Midianites would come in and take everything they had.

Gideon entered the scene. He tried to fool the Midianites so they wouldn't steal his grain by going to a winepress, pretending to be pounding grapes with his feet, when in reality he was grinding meal with which to make bread. When the angel of the Lord came, Gideon was sneaking around and afraid. Yet the angel addressed him as a "mighty warrior." I like that!

Gideon was told in no uncertain terms what God wanted him to do. God wanted Gideon to "go . . . and save Israel"—to pick up his sword and defeat the Midianites. All the details weren't told to Gideon, but he knew what God had in mind for him to do.

However, the enemy was fierce and had been around a long

time! So Gideon began to ask, "God, are You sure You have the right guy? Are You positive it wasn't someone else You wanted? Maybe Your angel got lost or something. Look at me, Lord. I'm the *least*—a nobody."

He didn't know then that a nobody is always somebody with God.

And God called this weak, scared "nobody" a "mighty warrior."

Yes, Gideon knew what it was God wanted him to do. He didn't need further direction. His need was for assurance! So he asked, "*If* now I have found favor in your eyes, give me a sign that it is really *You* talking to me" (v. 17, author's italics).

God proceeded to assure him! After asking that the angel wait, Gideon prepared food. "The angel of the Lord touched the meat and the unleavened bread. Fire flared from the rock, consuming the meat and the bread. And the angel of the Lord disappeared" (v. 21). Amazing! A consuming fire and a disappearing act.

But one miracle wasn't enough for Gideon. After taking a few feeble steps of obedience, a few days later an unsure Gideon began to have more doubts. He was so human! Gideon prayed, "If You will save Israel by my hand as *You* have promised—look, I will place a wool fleece on the threshing floor. If there is dew only on the fleece and all the ground is dry, then I will know that You will save Israel by my hand, as *You said*" (vv. 36-37, author's italics).

There was no doubt in Gideon's mind what God had told him, but he needed two more signs before he was convinced that God was the One speaking and would do as He said. First, he asked for wet fleece on dry ground, and then dry fleece on wet ground (vv. 39-40). God did both miracles graciously and without anger.

Some people use a similar method to determine *direction* from God. But if it is used at all, it must be remembered that

Gideon's example shows it should be used only to assure us that God has directed by other means.

Be careful with this one, friends. I am not saying you should never use it, but only use it with care, and use it the way Gideon used it.

Years ago I was forced to make a study of Gideon when circumstances were such that I was extremely tired of "living by faith." Things had gone from worse to worser. The ministry seemed to have collapsed. Finances were nil. Our friends had turned against us (or so it seemed). I came to the place where I breathed a deep sigh and said, "Lord, I've had it!"

About that time a job was offered me which was another one of those "fantastic opportunities"—hard to pass up. The job had a good salary, plus unlimited opportunities to work with college kids, settle down in one place, and not have to travel. What more could we want?

I went to a motel to try to find out what God wanted us to do. I began to read the Scriptures, but I didn't even know where to start so I just began catching up on my reading program. I read and read—through Jeremiah (which didn't encourage me too much!), then Lamentations (that was even worse!). The next book my program called for was 1 Chronicles, and when I got to chapters 12 and 13, several verses caught my attention. When I tried to read on, God brought me back to those verses. It seemed as though God was speaking to me and to my situation. But when I got down on my knees and said, "Lord, it looks like You are trying to say something to me here," my mind rejected it, saying, "No, I don't think so." Because if I was hearing correctly, God was saying I should stay with The Navigators and the fact was, deep in my heart, I didn't want to do that. The other job looked so much easier—so much better. Finally I came to the place where I said, "Lord, I don't know if You are speaking to me from this particular passage or not, so what should I do?"

It was then I remembered Gideon and the idea of a fleece. I needed to be sure of what I was doing, so I studied his story thoroughly and came to the conclusions I have shared—that there was no doubt in Gideon's mind as to what God wanted him to do. He didn't need direction—He needed assurance that God was speaking to him. And that was exactly what I needed. I didn't have the faith to step out and say, "OK, God, You have said it, so I'm going to do it."

So I asked God to do three things. I "put out a fleece." I asked that all three would happen within the next five days. And within five days, all had transpired.

Neither Gideon—who really did turn out to be a "mighty warrior"—nor I were ever bawled out for asking three things of God for assurance. But there are guidelines for the careful use of this method of God's guidance:

1. Use it prayerfully. Be convinced God would be pleased to have you proceed this way. Be careful you aren't "testing God" presumptuously.

2. Use it only for assurance that God has directed and not for the direction itself.

What Else?

Two other important considerations in finding God's will need to be mentioned:

1. God's Word. Obviously in most matters, the leading from God's Word would be foremost. Even in the gray areas, we can still go to the Scriptures. Many times as we open the Word, God will give us a passage for direction in that particular circumstance. Even though it may be out of context, as we pray over it and think about it, God makes it applicable to the very situation we are in. He *may* use His Word this way. But again He may not. That is His choice.

2. The counsel of godly people. "Where there is no guidance, a people falls, but in an abundance of counselors there

is safety" (Prov. 11:14, RSV) and "Without counsel plans go wrong, but with many advisers they succeed" (15:22, RSV) show us clearly that God guides through counselors.

Godly counsel can be used in two ways. One is just to seek counsel and get the wise guidance of godly people and then withdraw, spend time alone with God comparing what they have said with what God is speaking to you about according to Scripture. In this case their counsel may or may not be followed in your decision.

The other way of seeking godly counsel is for God to lead you to specific counselors whom you trust will give you the guidance of God and you will accept their counsel as His will. In this case you would pray, "Lord, lead me to three people whom I know and respect. I will heed their combined counsel and believe their advice will reveal Your will to me."

Now a word about some things to be careful of in determining God's will. We should not place an undue value on:

1. Circumstances. Circumstances *can* play a part in finding God's will, but there are times when they may not play any part at all, as was the case of my job in Chicago. God may want us to go forward even if a door looks completely closed. We go forward by faith, knowing His timing is perfect. Then, like a door-opener at the supermarket which only opens when you are *there*—the split second before you walk right into the glass—the situation will conform to God's leading.

The hardest thing in the world for some of us is to *wait*. Yet the Scripture often encourages us to do just that (Isa. 30:18; 40:31). We want to jump on the thing that is most obvious, the easiest. But we need to be willing to wait patiently until God has clearly revealed His will. Then we "will know the proper time and procedure" (Ecc. 8:5-6). Every decision not only has a "way" or direction, but it also has a time. I have known people to do the right thing within the scope of God's will, but either prematurely or late.

2. Money—or lack of it—is a peculiar circumstance that is used by many to try to determine what God would have them do. "I can't afford to go to that conference" or "Where will I get the money to do that job?" are words frequently heard. If God "owns the cattle on the thousand hills, the wealth of every mine" as the song goes, can He not provide the resources needed to do His will?

3. Ungodly counsel should not be heeded. "Blessed is the man who does not walk in the counsel of the wicked or stand in the way of sinners or sit in the seat of mockers" (Ps. 1:1). Some need to be aware that taking advice from a non-Christian psychologist, teacher, or relative may be entirely wrong.

The bottom line in determining God's will is to have a heart that is completely open to do anything He wants us to do. From our viewpoint, we may see several ways to go. From God's viewpoint, He sees one—perhaps a different one than any we see.

But as we seek His Word, His peace, His godly counsel—as we are conformed to His way of thinking through the Scriptures—He promises us in ringing tones, "I will instruct you and teach you in the way you should go" (32:8). Being taught by Him is a good thing and we are promised, "For the Lord God is a sun and a shield; He bestows favor and honor. No good thing does the Lord withhold from those who walk uprightly"(84:11, RSV).

9

Take
Heed to Yourself

Eric, age three and a half, was laughing as he perched on a pile
of rocks beside the hotel's kiddie pool. His grandmother and I
were supposed to be keeping an eye on him and we should
have warned him that his position was precarious. Suddenly
a frantic, fearful look creased his face. He lost his balance, fell
over backward, hit his head on a rock, and began to scream.
And no wonder. Within seconds a very large lump appeared on
his cranium. We tried in vain to comfort him.

God often tells His children, "Watch out!" Over a dozen
times the phrase is used, "Take heed to yourselves" (KJV) or
"Watch out," "Guard yourselves," "Be careful." Unlike our
unspoken warning to Eric, God's instructions are loud and
clear, coming in time to prevent catastrophe.

Negative Commands

With few exceptions, God's commands are warnings *not* to do
something. He told the Israelites not to touch the mountain, not
to make a treaty, not to provoke the people, not to become

111

corrupt, not to forget the covenant, not to be enticed to turn away from God.*

While many of God's warnings were aimed specifically at the Israelites, others are more general and apply to believers in all ages. But we, like the Israelites, continue to violate God's commands.

The Lord Jesus said, "Be careful, or your hearts will be weighted down with dissipation, drunkenness, and the anxieties of life" (Luke 21:34). Paul warned, "Watch your life and doctrine closely. Persevere in them, because if you do, you will save both yourself and your hearers" (1 Tim. 4:16). Perhaps one of our most flagrant transgressions as a nation is against the reproof found in Malachi 2:15-16: "So guard yourself in your spirit, and do not break faith with the wife of your youth. 'I hate divorce,' says the Lord God of Israel, 'and I hate a man's covering himself with violence as well as with his garment,' says the Lord Almighty. So guard yourself in your spirit and do not break faith." With the divorce rate approaching the 50 percent mark in the United States, it is obvious that as a nation we have not guarded ourselves in our spirits.

We should guard the sanctity of marriage because of its value. So too our hearts, our lives, our beliefs. God tells us to *watch* our lives and beliefs closely, to be *careful* of our hearts, to *guard* our marriages.

And what we're guarding is not junk. As the saying goes, "God don't make no junk."

Garbage Removal

We are valuable to God Himself. Often, however, we have to do some internal housekeeping to clean out the garbage of sin we've accumulated before we see the need to guard ourselves. Then, when the garbage is hauled away and the house of our

---

*Exodus 19:12; 34:12; Deut. 2:4; 4:15–16, 23; 11:16.

lives is restored, we begin to actively guard the house. So a prior step in "taking heed to ourselves" is God's command to purify or cleanse ourselves. "Since we have these promises [of God being our God, 2 Cor. 6], dear friends, let us *purify ourselves* from everything that contaminates body and spirit, perfecting holiness out of reverence for God" (2 Cor. 7:1).

When I read this, I thought, "Now wait a minute! I am purified by the washing of regeneration—the blood of Christ cleanses and purifies me." True. *Positionally* I stand holy and blameless before God because of the sacrifice of Christ who paid the penalty for all my sin. But *practically,* in everyday life, I need to open myself to the cleansing of God's Word and His Spirit day by day. How do I do that? James (4:8) tells me: "Come near to God and He will come near to you. Wash your hands, you sinners, and purify your hearts."

The other day I noticed that the drain in our upstairs shower wasn't draining at all well. Water stood for quite some time before disappearing ever so slowly, leaving a gray scum behind. Even though I scrubbed the tub, faucet, and drain top carefully, the problem remained. Drano helped very little.

Finally I removed the chrome top and stuck a coat-hanger wire down the drain. Yuk! What a lot of junk had collected just below the surface. I pulled out blobs of hair and dirt, poured Drano to clean out the rest, and finally the drain began acting properly.

This is so like my life. It may be carefully cleaned and polished on the outside, but just beneath the surface is a lot of gunk. (Believe it or not, that word is in my dictionary. It means "any oily, viscous or thick, messy substance. Perhaps from *goo + junk*.") At such times the free-flowing Spirit of God which should wash me through continually is hampered. I am virtually useless in fulfilling the purpose for which I was created. Sometimes it takes a drastic cleansing from God, a willingness on my part to let Him clean below the surface even if it means using a sharp instrument to cut away the filth. Willing-ness. That's the key. My part is to pry off the lid of my life—or at least be willing to let it be pried off by another person and/or the Holy Spirit so the dirt can be exposed to God's instrument of cleansing.

On a daily basis we purify ourselves through a daily cleans-ing of the Word. John (15:3) tells us, "You are already clean because of the word I have spoken to you," or "Cleansing . . . by the washing . . . through the Word" (Eph. 5:26, KJV). If we walk around a bonfire, we will come away smelling like smoke. In the process of walking through the world, all kinds of impuri-ties cling to us and we need the daily cleansing of God's Spirit through His Word.

But often we need *special* cleansing or purification—we need a sharp instrument to expose and dig away at the filth that's blocking the unhampered outpouring of God's Spirit in our lives. Our response to His revealing us to ourselves should be confession of all that's been hindering. Confession cleanses.

David, after sinning with Bathsheba, was completely devas-tated by what he had done and poured out his heart before the Lord. He said:

> Have mercy on me, O God,
>   according to Your unfailing love;
> according to Your great compassion
>   blot out my transgressions.
> Wash away all my iniquity
>   and cleanse me from my sin.
>
> For I know my transgressions,
>   and my sin is always before me.
> Against You, You only, have I sinned
>   and done what is evil in Your sight,

so that You are proved right when You speak
and justified when You judge.
                                              Psalm 51:1-4

The affair with Bathsheba and the murder of her husband
Uriah, so David could make his child legitimate, was a giant
block in God's blessing David. He had to expose his sin and let
God deal with it.

David began by begging God for *mercy*. Usually we need to
begin that way too. God knows what kind of people we really
are. He knows the blackness of our hearts, the pride, jealousy,
irritation, and bad attitudes that creep into our thoughts even
when they don't show themselves to others. I need to have God
"wash away all my iniquity and cleanse me from my sin"
(v. 2). The King James Version says, "Wash me throughly"—
all the way through.

Cleansing is the only healthy way to deal with sin. If I keep
the sin to myself and hide it, a terrible thing happens which is
described graphically in Psalm 32:3: "When I kept silent, my
bones wasted away through my groaning all day long. For day
and night Your hand was heavy upon me; my strength was
sapped as in the heat of summer."

Confession means admitting we have wronged God. David
wanted a sweet spirit, but he didn't have it until he had confessed and then prayed, "Create in me a pure heart, O God, and
renew a steadfast spirit within me" (Ps. 51:10).

God not only desires to unclog our *giant* blockages of sin. He
also wants to get rid of all *small* pieces of dirt which cling to
the valves and pipes of our lives. He may point out a sin of
neglect—something we are not doing that we should be doing.
Scripture tells us that "Anyone, then, who knows the good he
ought to do and doesn't do it, sins" (James 4:17). The sin may
be negligence of God's Word, a failure to pray, or a complacen-
cy in sharing Christ. "Sin is my claim to my right to myself,"
defines Oswald Chambers.

God wants complete access to my life—not "almost" access. It is when we are especially sensitive to God's voice—unusually attuned to Him—that He begins to work at the floating pieces of dirt that can keep us from being clean channels. We need to pray for God's searching light because our hearts are deceitful and the easiest person to fool is oneself. Jeremiah tells us, "The heart is deceitful above all things, and desperately wicked" (17:9, KJV), and I have to echo, "How true!"

When we lived in Portland, there was a time when my fellowship with God was uniquely sweet. On my knees before the Lord one morning, I prayed Psalm 139:23-24: "Search me, O God, and know my heart; test me and know my anxious thoughts. See if there is any offensive way in me, and lead me in the way everlasting." Suddenly God brought something to my mind that almost shocked me into standing straight up!

One time in seminary, I found myself unprepared for a Hebrew exam (I hated Hebrew!), so I cheated on that exam. Yes, I was a seminary student preparing for the ministry but that is what I did.

I had completely forgotten about that incident until I was on my knees before God asking Him to *search* my heart. This wasn't a time that I was *out* of fellowship with God—indeed I was in sweet fellowship with Him which is probably what caused me to open my heart and hear His voice so distinctly.

There is only one thing to do when God brings a sin to your remembrance and that is to confess it. So I confessed to God the fact that I had cheated on that exam.

The next morning as I came to the Lord to open His Word and pray, the same thing came back again. I thought, "Well, Lord, I thought I had that squared away with You yesterday morning." But I couldn't forget it. And every time in the next few days when I got down on my knees to pray, God would bring this thing to mind.

I began to wonder if there was more the Lord wanted me to

do. Finally, as much as I hated to admit it, I knew exactly what the Lord wanted me to do. He wanted me to write the president of the seminary and admit that I had cheated.

I wanted to say, "Now wait a minute, Lord. I have come to You in the light of 1 John 1:9, that if I confess my sin, You are faithful to forgive and cleanse me from all unrighteousness. I have it all straight with You. Why this?"

But I couldn't get away from the fact of His still, small voice—His *insistent* still, small voice—telling me what to do.

Finally I sat down and wrote a letter to the president of the school, telling him what I had done. I told him I had confessed this to the Lord, that I knew it was wrong, and I felt I should let him know so that he could take whatever action he thought necessary.

I put the letter in an envelope, addressed it, stamped it, and set it on my desk. The next morning I said, "Lord, look what I've done! You know my heart. I'd be willing to mail this if You want, but I've gone to all the trouble of writing this letter and my heart is right on it. Isn't that enough?"

No. It wasn't. That thing didn't leave my heart until I dropped the letter in the mailbox. Then a weight rolled off my life.

Forgiveness and Purification

One day toward the end of his father's life, Dr. Irwin Moon, creator of the Moody Science Films, asked, "Dad, if you could leave me with just one verse of Scripture that stands out to you above all others that I could take through my lifetime to apply day after day, which verse would you leave with me?"

Without a second's hesitation, Daddy Moon—a true saint of God—looked his son right in the eye and said, "Son, there is a verse that I use every day on this earth and it is, 'If we confess our sins, He is faithful and just and will forgive us our sins and purify us from all unrighteousness' " (1 John 1:9).

Confession results in *changes*—changes in our lives, in our ministries, in our relationships with God Himself.

In our lives the results are dramatic. Instead of sorrow, the joy of our salvation. Instead of confusion, wisdom. Instead of impurity, a clean heart and a steadfast spirit. Instead of emptiness, a consciousness of God's presence. Instead of fear, a knowledge that God is upholding us (Ps. 51:8, 6, 10-12).

In your ministry, the rewards of confession will be a fruitful life (v. 13). When you confess and are cleansed, you have fresh freedom and liberty in witnessing. No longer can Satan accuse you by saying, "How can you tell another about Christ after you have done that?"

Finally, after you confess your sins your relationship with God is affected and you again have a heart of praise (v. 14). Your "sacrifices and burnt offerings" are worthless unless—until—your heart is right before God. You may go to church, be faithful in prayer meeting, do all the right things in church and community. You may even have a devotional time, memorize Scripture, do Bible study, but it will mean *nothing* if you do not have a broken spirit—a broken and contrite heart before God (v. 17).

God is interested in the attitudes of our hearts. When my heart is pure—washed clean by confession—then my actions will show it. But all my "doing" is useless without my *being* right with God.

Humility

Following close on the heels of God's command to purify ourselves is His strong admonition to humble ourselves. We may think of humility as a Mr. Milquetoast but humility is more like Mr. Atlas. It takes strength to be humble!

I laughed and hurt at the same time as I read this account in a friend's letter:

Several months ago in a large mall department store, my wife found a $23 pair of slacks—just what she had been looking for for months—and on sale for just $12.

As she stood examining the garment, a lady walked up and said, "Here, let me help you," taking the slacks out of her hands. Then as the woman walked toward the dressing room, she said, "If they don't fit me, you can have them."

Jeri was stunned—she could hardly believe her eyes and ears! Since the lady didn't return, Jeri concluded that they had "fit" and that the woman had paid for them and taken them home.

For two days Jeri battled depression over the disappointment. As we discussed the situation, we both came to the conclusion that meekness is perhaps one of the most difficult of Christlike traits to develop.

Someone has defined meekness as "the attitude that submits to God's dealings without rebellion and to man's unkindnesses without retaliation."

Meekness is not repression—it is claiming the power from God to exercise love and self-control. It is *choosing* not to take justice into our own hands when everything within our Adamic nature is screaming for revenge.

Several months later Jeri had another opportunity. This time she was standing in a supermarket checkout line with only a couple of items in her hands. A middle-aged lady with a grocery cart pulled up—not behind her—but alongside her.

After a couple of minutes, Jeri felt a tap on her shoulder and turned to hear the lady ask in a gruff tone, "Are you in line?" When Jeri answered in the affirmative, the woman angrily replied, "Well, I'm ahead of you!"

There was a tremendous urge within Jeri to argue with the woman and "put her in her place." But all of a sudden, remembering the principle, Jeri said, "OK, if it is that important to you, go ahead." At which the woman said, "It is!" and pulled ahead without flinching.

This time instead of depression we both had a good laugh as Jeri came home and rehearsed the drama in the supermarket. It is true that grace is available in abundance if we speak the truth in love and then *choose* not to fight our own battles.

From the Word two principles seem to be the dynamic in developing meekness. One is setting our affections on things above and not on things on the earth—letting Christ be our one passion in life—so that everything else is of little consequence.

The second principle is believing that God loves to make up to us what other people owe us—if we look only to Him for the repayment. However, the unforgiving attitude we often have toward our "debtor" is a tipoff that we are still looking to men—and thus God's hands are tied.

The crucial issue then becomes, Who do I want "repaying" me—God, or the human being who has mistreated me?*

Humble yourselves—it's quite a project, isn't it?

The story is told of some children who worked long and hard on their own little cardboard shack. It was to be a special spot—a clubhouse—where they could meet in solemn assembly or just laugh, play games, and fool around. As they thought long and hard about their rules, they came up with three rather perceptive ones:

1. Nobody act big.

---

*Jim White's staff letter of November, 1978. Printed with permission.

2. Nobody act small.

3. Everybody act medium *

Humility is acting "medium." It isn't demeaning oneself or the opposite extreme of bragging. "Let another praise you . . . someone else, and not your own lips" (Prov. 27:2). Meaning what? Meaning no self-reference to some enviable accomplishment. Meaning no desire to manipulate and manufacture praise. Meaning authentic surprise when applauded. Meaning genuine, rare humility—regardless.†

At an awards reception, one of a group of reporters asked Corrie ten Boom, "Don't you have trouble keeping humble after being honored so greatly?"

Without hesitation, she answered, "When Christ was riding into Jerusalem and people were throwing palm branches in His way, crying all honor to Him, do you think the donkey thought it was for *him?* I am but a donkey and know these honors are for Christ alone."

However, humility does not consist in thinking cheaply of oneself.

There were some articles in *The London Times* on pollution which ended with the cry, "What's wrong with the world?"

An answer came: *Dear Editor: What's Wrong with the World?*
I Am.

> *G.K. Chesterton*

No, humility does not consist in thinking cheaply of oneself—or feeling that you are what is wrong with the world. Humility simply does not think of itself at all—but of Christ. It is knowing you are but "the donkey" and the honors are for the Lord.

---

*Taken from Leslie B. Flynn, *Great Church Fights* (Wheaton: Victor Books, 1976, p. 105).
‡Swindoll, Charles, *Home Is Where Life Makes Up Its Mind.*

In order to insure that we walk before God with integrity of heart, we must constantly be on guard against the wiles of Satan—against the encroachment of the world—against the lust of our own flesh. Being "on guard" requires purifying ourselves by confession of sin and humbling ourselves under the mighty hand of God.

God's command rings in our hearts: "So *be very careful* to love the Lord your God" (Josh 23:11).

Be careful—it's the only life you have.

10

Lay up
Treasures of People

I was on my way, but I wasn't sure why! As I drove the miles from Portland to Salem, I puzzled over my decision, a bit concerned with what I was letting myself in for.

The year was 1956. I had been a youth director and assistant pastor in Portland for only a short time when a girl I had known in college urged me to go to a Navigator conference that was being held in Salem.

I had heard Dawson Trotman, founder of The Navigators, speak once or twice. But The Navigators was a rather small organization at that time and I couldn't figure out why I should go to one of their conferences.

All I knew about The Navigators was that they had a memory program and I was a bit afraid that a Navigator conference might consist of sitting around reviewing verses. I knew I couldn't compete!

But there I was headed toward Salem on a gloomy Saturday morning to attend the morning session of a weekend conference.

What I heard that morning was the beginning of some dramatic changes in both my life and in Carole's, eventually changing the whole direction of our ministry.

One on One

Just before lunch some young men spoke—each taking a couple of minutes to tell about the personal ministry he was having in the life of *one* other man. These men were from all walks of life—a businessman, a serviceman, a young pastor, a doctor. One told about leading a friend to Christ and helping him begin a daily devotional time, teaching him how to study the Bible, how to memorize Scripture, how to share his testimony and the Gospel. The friend had recently led someone else to Christ and was beginning to follow up on him in the same way.

I had never heard anything before concerning personal follow-up—one person helping just one other person—and I was deeply impressed. I had been through college and seminary but most of what I had learned about the Christian ministry had been geared for groups rather than for individuals. I had learned little of a positive, aggressive nature on how to help *one* person grow spiritually on an individual basis.

The criterion for success in working with groups seemed to be the bigger the group, the more successful you were. Because we were having a certain degree of response in our young people's program, we were "successful."

But the thought of having a ministry with one individual and teaching him to pass on those principles both bewildered and intrigued me.

The next Sunday evening Skip Gray, a Navigator representative, was speaking to our college-age young people. His talk was practical and challenging; simple, yet profound. He had a grasp of the Word which years of education had not given me. I invited him to lunch the following Tuesday.

As we ate and talked, unintentionally Skip embarrassed me.

When I would try to use a verse of Scripture, invariably I quoted it incorrectly and of course, had no idea where it was found. Quietly, Skip would say, "Oh, you mean . . ." and he would quote the verse word-perfect and add its reference!

About the fourth time this happened, he pulled out a little packet which had four verses in it. He asked me if I'd ever seen one of them before.

"No," I responded. (I had been shown 108 verses in one fell swoop by a student in dining hall line in college, but I hadn't seen just 4.)

"Well, this is a way to begin memorizing Scripture," he said.

Skip took at least 10 minutes to explain the purpose of memorizing Scripture and the importance of those particular four verses in our battle against the spiritual forces of evil.

Then he casually leaned over the table, took the packet from me, put it in his shirt pocket and said, "Now Jack, if you want to memorize these verses, all you have to do is ask me for this packet."

At that, I was more than embarrasssed. Here I was a seminary graduate and this guy was giving me a little routine about memorizing verses on cards. My pride welled up within me and I thought, "Nuts to you, Buddy!"

But God wouldn't let me live with that attitude and in a few minutes I asked Skip for the verses and that week I memorized all four.

The next week we got together again and Skip gave me another group of eight verses. He began to share with me other practical ways for intake of God's word, as well as methods to make them pass-on-able—easily shared with other individuals.

My intention when I started was to learn to help others, but what I learned changed *me*.

As my walk with the Lord deepened, the passion for helping people individually began to grip my whole life. I was like a tiger waiting to pounce on any innocent who came to me or who I heard wanted spiritual help to learn how to grow. My inexperience caused me to make a lot of mistakes, but I also learned a great many lessons. I became convinced that the way to learn to work with people individually is to work with people individually. God is sovereign and He is going to make up for our errors. He will not let someone's life be ruined because of some dumb stunt we may ignorantly pull.

For four jampacked months, Skip helped me and then he moved to Dallas. I soaked in all the additional help I could get from Navigators in Salem, from conferences, and from anyone who knew how to work with individuals.

Job Switch

The next spring, Dawson Trotman came through Portland and stopped by our home. It was the first time I'd met him and in the course of an hour's conversation, he mentioned that someday he'd like to have us on the Nav staff. That was all he said at the time and we didn't give it much thought.

During these months, I began to experience unrest concerning my job. I felt we should do something else, but I didn't know what. I pursued everything from the pastorate to the mission field, but God never pushed the door open or gave us peace to move in these directions. Months after meeting Daws, God brought his statement to mind and I began to pray about it daily.

Finally I wrote a short two-paragraph letter to Daws saying in essence, "I am interested in the statement you made. Could we get together and talk about it further?"

A few days later, I received an invitation from Daws to come to Glen Eyrie, the Navigator headquarters in Colorado Springs, and spend a few days.

At Glen Eyrie, Daws spent a number of hours sharing his heart's vision. Then he invited Carole and me to join the staff. In view of needing to discuss with him in person other important considerations if we were to come on the staff, I felt that a decision needed to be made before I returned home in two days.

I will never forget that Thursday evening. Hosts of brilliant stars winked through wispy clouds, giving the only illumina- tion to the crisp, dark night as I began to walk the roads of Glen Eyrie to pray. My heart was in turmoil and frankly, I was scared. I knew so little of the organization, knew so few of the staff, knew nothing of what I would be doing.

I prayed, "Lord, should we come with the Navs? Should we leave the ministry in Portland to venture into this unknown territory? Please tell me what You want." As I continued to pray, an overwhelming sense of peace flooded my heart. Be- yond any doubt, I *knew* what God wanted us to do. He wanted us to come with The Navigators. Joyously, I began to sing and quote Scripture and all the night sounds murmured approval.

Completely at peace, I went back to my room and slept like a baby. The next morning I told Daws about my decision. (Lest any readers think Carole wasn't a part of this decision, the night before I flew to Colorado, she and I were lying in bed talking about the possibility of changing jobs and moving. She said, "Honey, I want you to know that however God leads you, I'm with you 100 percent." So I went to Colorado knowing that Carole would be with me in whatever God led me to do. I thank God for a wife like that!)

When I told Daws we wanted to be a part of The Navigators, he said, "Great! I sort of sensed this would happen. We would like to have you and Carole go to Long Beach, California and for you to take over the directorship of the Long Beach Service- men's Center."

I said, "Daws, I've never been in the service. I don't know anything about servicemen. I don't even know their ranks—I wouldn't know what to *call* a guy when he walked in with all those hashmarks on his sleeve, let alone anything about running a servicemen's center. What I need is *training.* I need to come here to the Glen and get *trained.*"

He said, "No, several of us have discussed it and prayed about it, and we've decided that you should go to Long Beach."

I said, "But Daws ..." and went into my long argument again.

In an "arguments-won't-help" tone, he responded, "Look, Jack, *you know enough to start.*"

Well, I couldn't argue with that. I did know enough to start. Two months later, we packed up all we owned in a U-Haul trailer and headed for Long Beach.

That sounds simple, doesn't it? But it wasn't!

One of the problems we faced was with some close, well-respected friends who warned us *against* The Navigators and counseled us strongly not to go on the staff. They warned us that The Navigators would try to run our lives, and force people we didn't know to live in our home.

We have been with the Navs many years now and found those accusations to be totally untrue. But at the time, they did have us wondering! And on our very first ministry assignment, we moved into a home with four fellows, a couple, one girl, and a dog—all of whom we didn't know. They didn't move in with *us*—we moved in with *them,* so it wasn't quite what our friends had warned us about—but it was close! However, we weren't forced to do this. Each step of the way, we were first asked to pray and consider. If God at any point didn't give a green light, it was agreed that it shouldn't be done.

But in the face of our friends' strong advice, we had to cling tightly to what we knew was God's leading. If we had listened to our friends, we would have missed the great privilege of investing our lives *individually*—to lay up for ourselves the treasures in heaven of *people.* I don't mean that we could not have done this within another church or organization—many Christians around the world are doing this very thing in different occupations—but for us the heart for working with individuals, the vision to multiply our lives, and the know-how for doing this very thing, had yet to be cemented and built into our own lives in such a way that we could invest in others.

God's Word and People

There are two things on this earth—right here and now—which are going to last forever. The Word of God. And people.

The Lord Jesus said, "Heaven and earth will pass away, but My words will never pass away" (Luke 21:33). He also proclaimed, "For God so loved the world that He gave His one and only Son, that whoever believes in Him shall not perish, but have eternal life" (John 3:16).

Why is it that even when I am aware of these two lasting, eternal entities, I give so much of my time to transient, inconsequential chores? Why do I allow the urgent interruptions, the frivolous demands, the insignificant trivia, to rob my day of the important, everlasting elements?

In those early days with Skip, I determined in my heart to begin to give at least a part of my day to that which will last forever—to the Word of God and to people.

We have discussed the fact that a disciple builds himself in the Word. I was beginning to make God's Word the foundation and structure in my life.

But what about the other "eternal"—people? As I examined my life, I saw more surface than depth in helping people grow to the maturity of becoming real followers of the Lord. I knew this needed to be done on a one-by-one basis.

God is interested in me—in you—as *individuals.* He calls us by our names. He knows the numbers of hairs on our heads. He knows our every thought.

Christ spoke to crowds. But He healed individuals.

And God deals with us one by one.

Dr. Edman said it well:

When God wants to drill a man,
And thrill a man,
And skill a man,
When God wants to mold a man
To play the noblest part;
When He yearns with all His heart
To create so great and bold a man
That all the world shall be amazed,
Watch His methods, watch His ways!
How He ruthlessly perfects
Whom He royally elects!
How He hammers him and hurts him,
And with mighty blows converts him
Into trial shapes of clay which
Only God understands;
While his tortured heart is crying
And he lifts beseeching hands!
How He bends but never breaks
When his good He undertakes;
How He uses whom He chooses,
And with every purpose fuses him;
By every act induces him
To try His splendor out—
God knows what He's about!*

*From *The Disciplines of Life,* © 1982 Harvest House Publishers, 1075 Arrowsmith, Eugene, OR 97402.

11
Lay up Treasures of Disciples

On the top of a small mountain, the disciples gathered closely around Christ, sensing the urgency and importance of this moment. They were oblivious to the sun's warmth on their weathered faces. Their concentration was only on their Master.

For the last three years, they had followed Jesus along the dusty roads of Galilee and Judea, totally involved in His life and ministry. His death was recent history. Forty days before, they had experienced with awe the wonder of His resurrection. They had been a part of His frequent appearances in their midst. At this moment somehow they knew He was going to leave them and they would be left on their own. He had trained them for this time, imparting to them everything they needed to know to carry on the ministry He was leaving with them.

Now He gathered them together to give His final instructions. The Twelve, minus the one who had betrayed Him, stood waiting uneasily.

He spoke. "All authority in heaven and on earth has been given to Me. Therefore go and make disciples of all nations, baptizing them in the name of the Father and of the Son and of the Holy Spirit, teaching them to obey everything I have commanded you. And surely I will be with you always, to the very end of the age" (Matt. 28:18-20).

His last words on earth and He spoke assurance first! "All authority in heaven and on earth has been given to Me," Christ said. Jesus Christ was saying, "I am omnipotent—all-powerful. I control the direction and thrust of your lives and any obstacles you may face. I am able to move into any situation, overcome any problem. Always remember this."

Make Disciples

Next came the word, "Therefore" or "in light of that." His command to "go and make disciples" is only possible in light of the fact that Christ has all power and authority.

The Greek language is both rich and fascinating. When we look at the original language, we discover that there is only *one* true verb in this passage—it is the word for "make disciples."

The word translated "go" is an *aorist* participle—a verb form which modifies the true verb. The "go" is action that is antecedent to the main verb—an action that takes place before the action of the main verb. In other words, the "going'" is to be done before the action of making disciples.

When we compare this "going" with other Scriptures, we find it is talking about evangelism—spreading the Gospel of Jesus Christ. The first thing Christ is saying we must do is to go and spread the Good News regarding Christ's death on the cross for man's salvation. We can't make disciples until people are led to Christ.

Now it is not always necessary to go somewhere else geographically. At this moment in the sphere of our influence, whether it is a classroom, a job, or a neighborhood, our job is to tell people about Christ.

But the primary emphasis here is to "make disciples." The phrase "make disciples" is in the aorist imperative tense which means it is a command with no "if clauses," no loopholes, and it denotes an appeal to the *will*. It expresses neither probability nor possibility, but only intention—that is, "What do I intend to do about it?"

When the aorist imperative tense is used, it denotes summary action—action to be taken at once, without delay. Christ is saying, "Go and make disciples at once." This is not a request—it is an imperative command!

The words translated "baptizing" and "teaching" are participles—verb forms that denote the action takes place simultaneously with the making of disciples. In other words, part of the process of making disciples is to teach them or indoctrinate them. And what are we to teach them? To observe or obey all God's commands.

Teach Them to Obey

The words "teaching them to obey" are in the present infinitive—a present tense verb form in Greek which has the idea of continuous action in the present time, an action that is never to stop. The obeying is to start now and keep going forever.

Of all the things Christ could have said to the Eleven—the things that He wanted taught to future new disciples, it is interesting that He narrowed it down to just one thing. Think about that for a minute. He could have said, "I want you to teach these new disciples all the great doctrines of the Scriptures." Or "I want you to teach them how to be great preachers," or "I want you to teach them how to give their testimony and to witness." He could have admonished them to have a quiet time, memorize Scripture, study the Bible, or build churches.

Instead He simply said, "Teach them to *obey* My commands."

What was Christ driving at? He was saying plainly, "I want you to go and spread the Gospel. After some have come to know Me, I want you to concentrate on making them into disciples. A primary aspect of making them disciples is to teach these new disciples to *obey* all the commands I have given to you."

Why? Jesus Christ knew that if He could get people to become disciples and be obedient to His commands, all these other things would be done as well. We would have disciples who were saturated in the Word, who would spread the Gospel by testimony and witness, who would begin to build churches. All those commands are in His Word. If we can get people to *obey,* all else will be taken care of.

Four Study Tools

One of the simple tools for Bible study that I first learned from The Navigators is to take a verse, paragraph, or chapter and ask four questions concerning it:

(1) What does it say? (Check its content, either outlining, paraphrasing, or summarizing it.)

(2) What does it say somewhere else in Scripture? (The Bible is its own best commentary so this gives insight into its meaning.)

(3) What does it say that I don't understand? (Dig into its seeming problems.)

(4) And most importantly, What does it say to *me?* What does God want me to do about it?

Some people have all their biblical doctrine straight. They can argue effectively about the amillenial, premillennial, and postmillennial views and discuss intelligently the midtribulational, pretribulational, and post-tribulational views of the Rapture. But some of these same Bible scholars have never learned to walk around in the Scriptures in "shoe leather" Christianity.

Jesus Christ wants disciples who will place themselves under the authority of Scripture—people who will live with Him in such a way that whenever they are faced with everyday situations, problems, and temptations, their immediate response is, "What does the Bible say about this? What does God want me to do?" God wants people who immediately turn to Him for guidance rather than scheming, plotting, or trying to figure out in their own minds what to do.

The primary characteristic of a disciple of Jesus Christ is one who is *obedient* to the Scriptures.

It's a Command

Making disciples is a command. Part of the process of making disciples is to teach them to obey all the commands, including this last one in Matthew 28:19 which is, "Go and make [new] disciples." The 11 men who heard Christ's command began to do just that. They went out (the going) and preached the Gospel and many who heard received Christ into their lives. Then the Eleven began to teach these new Christians to obey all Christ's commands—including this last one which was to make disciples. After a few months of "going" and preaching the Gospel, some people that they preached to became believers. And they began teaching these new believers to obey all of Christ's commands—including this last one, to go and make other disciples.

Do you see the point? As we teach believers to obey all the commands Christ gave them, we *have to,* we *must,* include the command that Christ felt was so important that it was one of His last words He spoke before He went to heaven. The Eleven obeyed—and a chain was started that comes right down to you and me today. We are here as believers because they obeyed *all* of Christ's commands, including the one to "go and make disciples."

This is the task of each and every one of us. It is the task of a disciple. Then people become the "treasures" we lay up for ourselves in heaven (Matt. 6:20).

Prior to World War II, Dawson Trotman was living in southern California. He began a small ministry with some servicemen on board the battleship *U.S.S. West Virginia.* He was invited to San Diego by a woman and her daughter to meet some sailors they had in Bible study. These two women were concerned about a sailor from their church, Les Spencer, and asked Dawson to get in touch with him. So Daws looked up Les and they became friends.

One day about dusk, Daws and Les were parked in the hills above San Pedro Harbor praying and studying the Bible. A police officer walked up and, thinking they were up to no good, began to question them. Daws told him they were praying and reading the Bible. The officer wasn't used to that kind of answer!

Daws began to share the Good News of Jesus Christ with the policeman. Every time the officer brought up a question, Daws would take his Bible and turn to a passage or quote a verse that would answer that question. About an hour later the policeman bowed his head and received Christ into his life.

Les was impressed by this, especially the way Daws had used the Scriptures. As they were driving back down the hill, he said, "You know, I'd give my right arm to be able to do what you just did."

Daws responded bluntly, "Naw, you wouldn't."

Les replied, "Yes, I would. I really mean it."

Daws responded, "Naw, you wouldn't."

Les repeated firmly, *"Yes, I would!"*

Daws finally said, "OK, Les. It won't cost you your right arm, but there is a price to pay in being able to handle and use the Scriptures skillfully—a price of time and discipline."

So every time Les was off his ship, he and Dawson would spend hours together and Daws personally trained this new disciple in how to become obedient to the Word of God by teaching him how to memorize Scripture, how to study the Bible on his own, how to pray, how to have a devotional life, how to give his testimony and share the Gospel with a non-believer, and how to believe God in various areas of his life.

Les began to become an obedient disciple.

It wasn't long before Les brought a young sailor on board his ship to Daws and introduced him. "Daws, this is Gurney Harris," he said. "Gurney has recently come back to the Lord and wants to grow. I'd like you to teach Gurney all you've been teaching me."

Wouldn't you have been flattered by this? What would your response have been?

Daws answered, "Les, you teach him."

Les replied, "Oh, I can't do that."

Daws said flatly, "If you can't, then I've failed."

So, very feebly at first, Les began to share with Gurney how to begin to believe God, how to memorize and study the Bible, how to pray, how to share his faith. They had a quiet time together. They studied the Bible together. They began to witness together. They prayed together—just the two of them because that's the way Daws had done it with Les.

It wasn't long before Gurney came to Les with a guy by the name of John Dedrick in tow. John was an agnostic and it took six long months of watching Daws, Les, and Gurney before he came to Christ. Then he wanted to grow. Gurney asked Les, "Now that John has received Christ, will you teach him what you've been teaching me?"

What do you think Les said?

"You teach him."

Gurney responded, "Oh, I can't do that."

And Les' answer was, "If you can't, I've failed."

So Gurney began to teach John all that Les had taught him by doing those things together.

One man reached another man who touched another and this process began to grow—to mushroom—until at the end of World War II there were Navigators on over 1,000 ships and bases around the world. This process of multiplication was the beginning of the Navigator ministry and is the basis of its continuing today.

One man eventually reached was Howard Davis, a sailor who became a real disciple. When Howard got out of service, he wanted to finish college and went to a small midwestern school named Wheaton. While there he ran into a student by the name of Skip. Skip knew how to pray and each morning like clockwork, he would walk the streets of Wheaton praying. But he didn't know how to saturate himself in the Scriptures and was looking for a deeper walk with God. So Howard began teaching Skip and Skip soaked it in, grew in depth and knowledge, and eventually came on The Navigator staff.

One of Skip's first assignments was to help Youth for Christ in Portland, Oregon with a follow-up program.

Two or three months after Skip and his wife Buzzie moved there, they came into contact with a young man who had moved to Portland as a youth director in an evangelical church.

You know the rest of the story!

How is it that you and I can have a worldwide ministry for Jesus Christ? We personally may never go to the mission field, but a part of us can be working in a foreign land through someone in whose life we have invested.

Pass It On

And the beauty of it is every believer can do this. The definition of a disciple is a *learner,* so we need first to *learn.* But there is no Christian who hasn't something he can pass on to another person.

After I'd spoken on this subject one time, a guy came up to me and said, "Jack, I'm in the service and I really can't do *one* single thing."

I saw a *Beginning with Christ* packet sticking out of his shirt pocket. So I asked him, "Have you memorized the verses in that memory pack?"

"Yes, I've done that," he responded.

"Do you suppose you could help someone else memorize them?" I questioned.

"Well, yes, I suppose I could do that much."

"Have you memorized the next little packet?"

"I'm starting on it."

"Well, get somebody started and soon he'll be pushing *you* to keep ahead," was my advice.

I saw him a couple of years later, beaming from ear to ear. He'd taken on a dozen or so men who had pushed *him* to finish. He'd completed the Topical Memory System, done some Bible study books, and was really turned on for God.

A number of years ago a young couple graduated from the University of Missouri in pharmacy. The husband, who wanted to go into business for himself, heard about a little town in South Dakota named Wall that needed a pharmacy. So he and his wife moved up to South Dakota and started their own drugstore. But business was terrible. Wall was about a half mile off the highway going to the Black Hills. All day long traffic would whiz by from east to west and back, but no one stopped in Wall.

One day as he and his wife were talking, she mused, "If only we could get some of those cars to stop, maybe they would buy something."

In their backyard they had a deep well with wonderful ice-cold water in it. She had a thought and suggested to her husband, "Do you suppose if we advertised 'free ice water' that some people might stop for it?"

He laughed and said it couldn't hurt to try.

So that night they made some small hand-printed signs. He put them up on telephone poles several miles east and west. The signs read, "Free ice water. Wall Drug Store. Wall, South Dakota."

A few people actually stopped and rather embarrassed, asked

for their free glass of ice water. After getting it, they would generally buy a little something.

Encouraged, the pharmacist painted bigger signs and put them farther up and down the highway. More people stopped. More signs.

By 1956 (they began shortly after World War II), they were giving out 5,000 glasses of ice water a day. They expanded their pharmacy to a grocery store, souvenir shop, dress shop, etc. Today they are millionaires.

It all began with an idea. Then they started where they were, they used what they had, and they did what they could.

What do you have that God can use?

God will bless you if you help fulfill the Great Commission to make disciples of every nation. Just start where you are, use what you have, and do what you can.

12

Lay up Treasures by Making Christ Lord

There we stood in all our splendor at the entrance of the Penrose Room at the Broadmoor Hotel and the maitre d' wouldn't let us in!

It was our 26th wedding anniversary and I had made reservations for a special night out at our favorite place in Colorado Springs. I wore Carole's choice—a dark brown turtleneck and a camel jacket. She was in the long dress she had bought for our daughter's wedding.

But the man in charge kept shaking his head. He was saying, "Yes, Mr. Mayhall, we have your reservation, but I can't let you in without a tie."

I was incredulous. Colorado Springs is a casual tourist-type town and I wasn't aware that any place had a "tie and coat" dress code.

I protested, "But it's our 26th wedding anniversary. We live clear across town so it's impossible to go home and change clothes and this is the place we like best to eat."

He replied, "I'm sorry, sir, but the rules are you can't come into the dining room without a tie."

"But can't you make an exception?" I pleaded.

"I'm sorry, but I don't make the rules and the management says. . ."

"Well," I looked helpless and hopeless at the same time, "what can we do?"

"Well, sir, I could loan you a tie," and he reached under the counter for a supply.

"Wear a tie with a *turtleneck*?" I inquired aghast. "You've got to be kidding!"

He tried in vain to suppress a smile. "You might start a whole new style," he managed to say.

Well, you won't believe this, but I went into the men's room and put on that crazy tie. When I came out, Carole just about came unglued. She was laughing so hard it was all I could do to keep her from rolling on the floor.

I asked the maitre d', "Do I have to wear this tie all evening?"

He replied, "Mr. Mayhall, the rule is you have to have a tie on to get *in*. What you do after that is your affair."

So we followed him into the Penrose Room and he gave us the best table in the restaurant, facing the mountains. With my back to the other diners, I took off the offending tie, laid it on the seat beside me, and we had a most memorable evening!

The Cost

There are times when we are willing to look like fools to get what we want. But are we willing to look like fools for the sake of Christ? We don't mind being "fans"—which is short for fanatics—of baseball, football, or tennis. But let anyone call us a "fanatic" for Christianity and we begin to have problems.

Yet Christ said plainly, "If anyone would come after Me, he must deny himself and take up his cross daily and follow Me" (Luke 9:23). Have you ever thought about what the Cross *meant* to Jesus Christ?

On the night before His crucifixion, Christ sweat agonizing drops of blood as He faced the cross. He cried to the Father, "Father, if You are willing, take this cup from Me; yet not My will, but Yours be done" (Luke 22:42).

Christ knew fully what He was facing. Your eternity and my eternity were at stake, but in His humanity He shuddered at the terrible price. His physical suffering was only a small part. The worse agony was bearing the sins of the world. He who was perfect, spotless, sinless *became* sin. He was so filthy with our sin in the eyes of God that God the Father had to turn His face away from God the Son. That's when Christ cried out, "My God, My God, why have You forsaken Me?" (Matt. 27:46) The ordeal of having all our sins heaped on Him on the cross literally broke Christ's heart.

Looking toward what was facing Him the next day, Christ cried, "If there is any other way to get this job done, Father, let's find it! Nevertheless, not My will, but Yours be done."

There was no other way. The Cross of Christ meant doing *all* the will of God despite the enormous cost.

Jesus Christ came into the world to be the King of kings and the Lord of lords. As Paul wrote:

Now Christ is the visible expression of the invisible God. He existed before Creation began, for it was through Him that everything was made, whether spiritual or material, seen or unseen. Through Him, and for Him, also, were created power and dominion, ownership and authority. In fact, every single thing was created through, and for, Him. He is both the first principle and the upholding principle of the whole scheme of Creation. And now He is the Head of the body which is the church. Life from nothing began through Him, and life from the dead began through Him, and He is, therefore, justly called the Lord of all (Col. 1:15-18, PH).

The King

It has been rightly said, "If Christ is not Lord *of all,* He is not Lord *at* all." Making Christ Lord means that you are committing *everything* to Him. This is not a once-for-all-time deal. After you have made that initial commitment, there are going to be things God will put His finger on and say, "Give *that* to Me." This is called "growth." In order for you to be *His* subject, He must be *your* King.

The story is told about two novice chess players who obviously didn't know much about the game. (If you aren't familiar with chess, the object is to capture the other person's king.) While both of the novice players were looking elsewhere, an observer quietly removed one of their kings. They went on playing for nearly an hour before one of them realized that a king was missing!

Many people make moves, proceed with decisions, and plan strategy for their lives without realizing *they have no King.* Self becomes the center of their lives. The King is missing.

Jesus Christ wants all of us. He wants no rival for our affections, no refusal in our commitment, no retreat in our battle.

Christ spoke about discipleship to the multitudes in hard terms. He said:

If anyone comes to Me and does not hate his father and mother, his wife and children, his brothers and sisters—yes, even his own life—he cannot be My disciple. And anyone who does not carry his own cross and follow Me cannot be My disciple.

Suppose one of you wants to build a tower. Will he not first sit down and estimate the cost to see if he has enough money to complete it? For if he lays the foundation and is not able to finish it, everyone who sees it will ridicule him, saying, "This fellow began to build and was not able to finish."

Or suppose a king is about to go to war against another king. Will he not first sit down and consider whether he is able with 10 thousand men to oppose the one coming against him with 20 thousand? If he is not able, he will send a delegation while the other is still a long way off and will ask for terms of peace. In the same way, any of you who does not give up everything he has cannot be My disciple (Luke 14:26-33).

The feeling we get as we read these words is that Jesus Christ is not playing games. He wants people to be His followers who are committed, learning disciples. Three times He says that if you are not willing to pay the price, you cannot be His disciple. Being one of His is serious business.

No Rival

The first requirement of a disciple is for a person to "hate" his father and mother, wife, children, brothers, sisters, and even his own life.

This word "hate" is a relative term meaning to have preference for one person over another.* It doesn't mean we are to have animosity or bitterness toward the people mentioned here. Of course not. We know from other Scriptures that we are to love everyone, even our enemies. But the word is a strong comparison. It means that Christ should be so far out in front in your priorities that in relation to your love for Him, it is as though you "hate" everyone else. He isn't to be just a fraction ahead of your next love, but He should be running ahead in your life by a country mile. No one else should come in a close second.

And trailing the field should be *self*.

---

*The same word is used in Luke 16:13: "No servant can serve two masters. Either he will *hate* the one and love the other, or he will be devoted to the one and despise the other. You cannot serve both God and money." One cannot serve both the world and Christ at the same time—a choice has to be made of one over the other.

Christ will have no *rival* if we are His true disciples. Oswald Chambers put it, "I have no business in God's service if I have any personal reserve. I am to be broken bread and poured-out wine in His hands."

James and John had a cozy little setup. They were in the fishing business with Dad, making good money, and were prominent in their small community. Peter was also a partner and all three had it made.

Then Christ walked into their lives and said, "Come, follow Me . . . and I will make you fishers of men" (Mark 1:16-20; Luke 5:10).

They pulled up stakes. They left Mom, Dad, their future livelihood and security, and followed Jesus Christ. And He didn't even tell them what was in store for them. I imagine they had a lot of questions going through their minds. Today they might have asked, "What is the salary? What kind of Social Security program and retirement benefits are there? What are the implications of this? What exactly is my job description?" But instead, they simply *followed* Him.

No Refusal

God brooks no rival for our affections nor does He allow for any refusal in our commitment.

Two friends and classmates of mine at Wheaton were destined to impact my life.

Jim Elliott was the kind of guy that, had we taken a vote on the young man most likely to succeed, he would have won. Jim had a marvelous mind, was a good athlete, and an extremely gifted speaker. I have never heard a man his age open and expound the Word of God as Jim Elliott did.

Ed McCully, president of our senior class, missed part of our Senior sneak because he was in California participating in the Hearst Newspapers' National Oratory contest—which he won. On returning, he came roaring into the conference grounds in northern Wisconsin on the hood of a Ford to the acclaim of our whole class. Several of us put him on our shoulders, marched him around, then took him out on the pier and, just to keep him humble, dumped him in Lake Michigan! (We figured he could afford a cleaning bill with the money he'd just won.)

After college Ed went to law school. But after just one semester, God got ahold of his heart and said, "Ed, I want you on the mission field." Ed quit law school and took a one-year course at Biola where he met his wife. A year later, they were in Ecuador.

Jim, Ed, Nate Saint, and two others teamed up in Ecuador in order to reach a savage and pagan tribe for Christ. They began praying about how they might reach these Auca Indians who lived in remote and inaccessible jungle areas.

Nate Saint, the pilot, figured out an ingenius way to fly over the Auca villages in a circle, creating a vortex in which to let down a basket of gifts. The men were elated when one day the Aucas put a gift for them back into the basket.

After much prayer, they went in to contact these Indians face to face. Landing on a sandy beach along the Curaray River, the five got out, stood on the beach, sang, and prayed.

Within an hour all five lay dead, face down in the river with spears in their backs. They had given their lives to take the Gospel to a tribe of savages out in the middle of nowhere, whom no one even knew about.

The story made the headlines of newspapers all across our country. *Life* magazine featured an article about it. And many asked the question, "Why?"

These were not ordinary, average, run-of-the-mill men. They were extraordinary individuals who could have been highly successful in many other kinds of endeavors. But God wanted them in Ecuador and they knew it was the total will of God for them. Jim and Ed spoke an eternal yes to God's will and died at age 29.

Sometime in his senior year of college, in 1949, Jim Elliott wrote these words in his diary: "God, I pray Thee, light these idle sticks of my life and may I burn for Thee. Consume my life, my God, for it is Thine. I seek not a long life but a full one, like You, Lord Jesus." God answered that prayer.

Christ had no rival for the love of Jim, Ed, Nate, and the others. All had families they loved dearly, but Christ was first—way out in front. He is *Lord.*

No Retreat

There should be no rival for our affections, no refusal in our commitment, and no retreat—no looking back—in our battle and journey with God.

In the book *Marine,* about the Korean conflict, the story is told of Chesty Puller. Some of his marines were being replaced by army units. A young army lieutenant was getting his instructions from Puller as to what they were to do and Puller pointed out a particular hill they were to take. It was a treacherous assignment.

After the instructions, the lieutenant turned to Puller and asked, "Sir, what is our line of retreat?"

Puller calmly walked into the communications tent with the lieutenant trailing after him and told the commanding officer to get the artillery on the field phone. He spoke to the artillery post and said, "The lieutenant and his men are going up hill 309. Train your guns on that hill and if one man begins to retreat, open fire."

Turning to the lieutenant, Puller asked, "Does that answer your question?"

No retreat.

God has no plan for retreat. We are to renounce *all,* and not look back.

Do you remember the story of Demas? Demas deserted Paul because he loved this world (2 Tim. 4:10). Demas had been with Paul on one of his trips to Thessalonica. Perhaps he had seen a cute little blonde there or had talked with a group of flourishing businessmen who wanted to make him a partner and told him, "If you ever get tired of walking down dusty roads with Paul, why don't you come back here and join us? We're making piles of money. This is a nice town to settle down in." Perhaps it was the blonde *and* the business, but Paul said, "For Demas, because he loved this world, has deserted me and has gone to Thessalonica."

Can you picture Demas? He's married the blonde, lives in a penthouse apartment overlooking Thessalonica, and has two camels in the garage. He has everything the world has to offer. I can imagine Demas standing out on his balcony in a silk bathrobe with the lights of the city below, thinking about how it used to be with Paul—how they were thrown out of cities and into jails. It was a tough but exciting time.

All we really know about Demas is that he had fallen in love with the world. He didn't finish the course. He retreated. What a sad commentary to a life.

The need of the world is for men and women who have counted the cost and determined to pay the price to make Christ complete Lord of their lives—to do all the will of God.

No rival—no refusal—no retreat.

But Christ does not leave us with this challenge without telling us of the *reward:* "There is no one who has left house or brothers or sisters or mother or father or children or lands, for My sake and for the Gospel, who will not receive a hundred-fold now in this time, houses and brothers and sisters and mothers and children and lands, with persecutions, and in the age to come eternal life" (Mark 10:29-39, RSV).

Do you know what percentage a hundredfold is? It is 10,000 percent, which is what the Bible tells us will be our reward *now,* in this life. What does this mean?

In 1965 Carole and I found ourselves wandering the dark

streets in the Arab section of Jerusalem. Most shops were closed and shuttered but as we turned a corner, we spotted a light in a little store front, so we stopped to investigate. We were delighted to discover it was a Christian bookstore—not many in those parts.

As we chatted with the owner, I mentioned I was with The Navigators. His eyes lit up and he said, "Oh, do you know Mr. Waldron Scott?"

I said, "Sure, I know him well."

"How about Pete Angier?" he inquired.

"Yes," I responded. "We are good friends."

For the next half hour we chatted about how great it was to be Christians and what the Lord was doing through his ministry at the bookstore. We were halfway around the world; yet within minutes we had found not just a friend, but a *brother.*

I find this unique phenomenon true anywhere in the world. The minute I run into someone who is committed to Christ and loves Him, I have a bond that is closer than any human bond possible.

And "houses." We didn't know when we left "home" in Oregon that we'd have access to a 63-room castle at Glen Eyrie, but we do!

We have gained brothers and sisters, mothers and fathers, houses and lands a hundredfold.

Christ will have no rival, no refusal, no retreat, but in His love, the rewards in *this* life are fantastic. And in the age to come—eternal life!

The choice to be a disciple yields eternal dividends. And this choice rests with me.

The story is told of a boy who held a tiny bird cupped in one hand and covered by the other. He asked a wise old man, "Is the bird alive or dead?"

If the man said "Alive," the boy would crush the bird before he showed it to him. But if the wise man said "dead," the boy would release it alive.

The wise man looked long at the boy and then he said, "My son, the bird is in *your* hands."

The choice of making Christ *Lord* is in your hands. The determination to be a disciple rests with you.

Your hands—alone.